THE RUNNERS BOOK OF
TRAINING SECRETS

By Ken Sparks, Ph.D.
and Dave Kuehls, Senior Writer, **RUNNER'S** WORLD.

Rodale Press, Inc.
Emmaus, Pennsylvania

Notice

This book is designed to help you make decisions regarding your fitness and exercise program. It is not intended as a substitute for professional fitness and medical advice. As with all exercise programs, you should seek your doctor's approval before you begin.

Runner's World is a registered trademark of Rodale Press, Inc.

Printed in the United States of America on acid-free ∞, recycled paper ♻

Cover Designer: Acey Lee
Cover Photographer: John Kelly

Library of Congress Cataloging-in-Publication Data

Sparks, Ken.
    The runners book of training secrets / Ken Sparks and Dave Kuehls.
         p.   cm.
    Includes index.
    ISBN 0–87596–307–2   paperback
    1. Running—Training. I. Kuehls, Dave. II. Title.
GV1061.5.S637   1996
796.42—dc20   95–23769

Distributed in the book trade by St. Martin's Press

2   4   6   8   10   9   7   5   3   1   paperback

—— OUR MISSION ——
We publish books that empower people's lives.

RODALE BOOKS

To my wife, Debbie, daughter, Kelly, and son, Chad.
They have endured my training, celebrated my successes
and consoled me during my losses.
And to all runners everywhere.
—*Ken Sparks*

For my parents.
—*Dave Kuehls*

Contents

Foreword

No runner is better qualified to comment on the sport's training secrets than Ken Sparks. As a competitive runner for more than 35 years and an exercise physiologist since 1968, Ken gained his expertise both on the track and in the lab. His considerable knowledge of physiology and kinesiology has allowed him to design training regimens that have made him a world-class performer at distances from 800 meters to the marathon.

I first met Ken in the fall of 1966 at Ball State University in Muncie, Indiana, where I had recently arrived to establish the Human Performance Laboratory there. While I had stopped coaching to concentrate on research, I had been asked to provide workouts for the cross-country team. So every afternoon, Ken and his teammates would come to the lab to pick up my "prescription" for the afternoon's workout.

I had coached cross-country at the State University of New York at Cortland before coming to Ball State, but my knowledge of sports training was drawn from years of competitive swimming. Thus, I tended to focus on relatively high-intensity interval training—more suited for competing at 800 meters than for the 10-K distance of collegiate cross-country running. (I'm sure Ken and his teammates must have had some choice remarks for those workouts.)

In 1968 Ken's training took a 180-degree turn when Ed Winrow joined the lab. Winrow—one of the best marathoners in the country—became the Pied Piper of Muncie's distance runners, convincing one and all that long slow distance (LSD) was the way to train. Ken replaced his own high-intensity track workouts with 10- to 15-mile runs at eight to nine minutes per mile. He even attempted a few marathon races. But his wheels always seemed to drag, so to speak, at 18 to 20 miles.

Fortunately, Ken returned to the track and the event for which nature had designed him—the 800 meters—in the early 1970s. Subsequently, his training shifted yet again from LSD to high-intensity 200-meter intervals. At one point his father built him a motor-driven treadmill out of parts found around the family farm. The treadmill became (and still is) an integral part of Ken's training program. Such quality training helped Ken blossom into one of the nation's top 800-meter runners. He competed in the 1972 Olympic Trials and as a member of a world-record two-mile relay.

Over the years, Ken has experimented with a variety of training regimens. In light of his success as a world masters record holder at 800 and 1500 meters, it appears that Ken has found a great many training secrets that have enabled him to win at almost any distance he chooses. In this book he and co-author Dave Kuehls present the wisdom of dozens of elite runners who have so generously shared their insights regarding their training and competition.

While there is no "best" way to train, the information in this book may give you insights into your own training, as well as expert suggestions that may help you realize your full talents.

Dave Costill, Ph.D.
Human Performance Laboratory
Ball State University
Muncie, Indiana

Traits of a Serious Runner

When the gun goes off to start the Revco/ Cleveland 10-K each spring, in the field of 7,000 are elite runners from the United States, Kenya, Mexico, Great Britain, Australia and many other countries. They start at the front of the pack and wear name-brand outfits supplied by their sponsors. Behind them are the masses: social workers from Cleveland, lawyers from Akron, students from nearby universities...butchers and bakers and candlestick makers. They wear whatever was clean that morning—or whatever was lucky last year.

Running may be the only sport where anyone can directly compete against the world's best. We know that we won't ever be as fast as 1992 Olympic Marathon bronze medalist Lorraine Moller or world-class masters runner Nick Rose, but they make us wonder: What do they know that can help my running?

That's what this book is about. It's a look at how many elite runners train, so that you can learn their secrets—and get faster, too.

Whether a runner is Moller or Rose—or just a 42-minute 10-Ker from Cleveland—certain ingredients are critical to success. Do *you* have these traits?

Do you want to improve? All serious runners want to be the best they can be. This best may be winning a race or simply finishing, beating the best time for your age group or setting a new personal record. Desire cannot be taught—it has to come from within. Driven by accomplishments as well as failures, at the base level desire comes from pure love of the sport and is the primary key to success in both training and racing.

1

What motivates you? Closely linked with desire is motivation—the prod that drives us to finish a tough workout. When your motivation is low and you would rather take the day off, remind yourself why you want to improve.

Many serious runners stay motivated by asking themselves: Is my competition taking a day off? "I reaffirm my goals daily: I race to challenge myself, to break personal barriers, to know myself and to improve," says veteran runner Lorraine Moller.

Are you dedicated? Desire and motivation foster dedication—the commitment to get out there, rain or shine. Those who achieve their goals at a Saturday race don't just run on Saturday; they run Monday through Friday as well to make a good showing on race day. "I train very hard," two-time U.S. Olympic marathoner (1988 and 1992) Cathy O'Brien says flatly. "I feel it gives me both physical and mental strength. And when it's time to race, I'm ready to go out and race hard."

Are you confident? "When you step to the line, if you believe in your training program and your physical readiness, you will race well," says Steve Holman, a 1992 U.S. Olympian at 1500 meters. Confidence in yourself and in your training is built gradually. It comes from within, from the knowledge that you have put in the miles—say a three-month segment of good training leading up to a 5-K race. "Confidence will also help you relax and make racing more fun," Holman adds.

Can you take disappointment in stride? Every running career has gone through aches, pains, setbacks and bad races. In short, runners experience defeat in many different forms. It helps us keep our successes in perspective. And if all this has taught us anything, it's humility.

Runners know that though they may be on a hot streak, a defeat could be just around the corner in the form of an injury or a drop in performance level.

"There's always someone else out there doing more, someone who could beat me at one time or another," says two-time British Olympian Jill Hunter (3000 meters in 1988 and 10,000 meters in 1992). "I want to get the best out of myself today because I can't predict tomorrow."

Are you flexible? Each of us is unique—we respond differently to certain experiences and situations. Keeping this in mind, plan your training around your individual personality.

For example, Steve Spence, the 1991 World Marathon Championships bronze medalist and a 1992 Olympic marathoner, has a hard time

DEVELOPING A WINNING ATTITUDE

Desire, motivation, dedication and confidence combine to give us a winning attitude about running. But building these components is not as easy as it sounds. The running commitment affects our whole life. Hence, our daily running habits—training, rest and diet—have to be woven in with our other commitments to jobs, family and friends. Marathoner Don Janicki, husband, father of three and account executive at the Bank of Boulder, still finds time to train and race.

"It's tough," he says. "We really have to switch our schedules around. But that's what I have to do if I want to get my training in each day."

running at the crack of dawn—it's just the way he is. So instead of dragging himself out of bed for the first run of the day, he gets up, has breakfast, relaxes for a while and then, late in the morning, heads out the door to run. Finding the right training program for you is a key to running well.

Are you tuned in to your physical capabilities? Not everyone has the speed of Carl Lewis or the endurance of Frank Shorter, winner of the 1972 Olympic Marathon. Each of us has varying degrees of physical ability; the challenge is to take what we have and develop it to our fullest potential. A good training program maximizes our strengths and shores up our weaknesses. This requires planning and perseverance, but the rewards are worth it.

Dan Held, who won third place at the 1995 U.S. Marathon Championships, devotes most of his training to strength and endurance, not speed. Why? "I just don't have the speed of many of the other runners, and the only way I'm going to stay close at the end of a marathon is through strength," he says.

Goal-Setting: The Fundamental Ingredient

The traits we've been talking about are strongly linked to a runner's goals. Your reason for running could be to stay in shape, to control stress, to run in the annual Fourth of July 5-K or to lower your 10-K time from college. Goals motivate us, strengthen our dedication and put us on the road to running success.

Yet goal-setting can be tricky. The key is to set goals in steps and make them reasonable. If you've just run a 38:12 10-K in April, don't decide to aim for 34:30 by October. Make that your long-term goal, say in two or three years. This year, shoot for 37:00. Move too quickly and you will set yourself up for defeat, and that setback might discourage you in your running.

Goal-making can and should be fun. Be sure your goals are attainable, not so far out of reach or long term that your dedication wavers. Take a tip from NCAA 5000-meter champ Laurie Gomez-Henes, who ran her second 10,000-meter race in the 1993 U.S.A. Track and Field Championships (coming in fifth with 32:54, a personal record by 15 seconds): "I could've tried for a 32:20 and gone out fast and died and ended up hating the 10,000. A 32:50 was a much more reasonable goal. And I did it."

What You Can Learn from Top Runners

To achieve peak performance, you have to tailor your training to your goals, age, physical ability and personality. In other words, for best results, your program has to fit you well.

In this book you'll find the collective experience of over 50 world-class runners who tell you what works for them. Combined with these training secrets are the underlying scientific principles of training that explain why they work. Use this information to adapt and design your individual plan for success.

Plan your program around your goals first, and then work it around your schedule. Remember, life goes on, and running for most of us is not a chore but a hobby that should be enjoyed. Set your goals over at least a one-year period, dividing your training into seasons and shifting the emphasis, as needed, to base work, strength development, speedwork or competition. Don't be in a rush to compete before you're ready.

You may not be an Olympic runner, but there's no reason why, on a smaller scale, you can't train like one. "There are no shortcuts to distance running success," says Bob Kennedy, a 1992 U.S. Olympian at 5000 meters. He outlines a simple three-step process: "First, you have to put in the work. Second, you have to believe in the system you train under. Third, you have to get out and perform when it matters."

This book will help you tackle all three.

Physiological Profile of a Runner

Yale law student Frank Shorter, with a black mustache and an insouciant expression, crosses the finish line to win the 1972 Olympic Marathon. This was a seminal moment in the popularity of distance running. Before Shorter's triumph—on national television and with best-selling author Erich Segal screaming out commentary—most people thought running was a sport reserved for geeks and loners. Shorter brought the sport out of the woods—onto the roads and into the parks of America. The running boom was born.

The profile of a good distance runner, such as Shorter, is complex and involves heredity, anatomy, physiology and psychology. Over the years scientists have poked, probed and sometimes almost tortured elite athletes to find out what makes them tick. These studies have given us insight into the physiological makeup of a distance runner and have laid the foundation for better and more efficient training methods.

Identifying Your Potential

Each of us has the potential to perform at a certain level. Keep in mind, however, that not everyone can become an Olympic champion; even though we all will improve by training, each person comes from a specific genetic makeup and so has unique innate abilities. Shorter has different abilities than Bill Rodgers, who is different from Alberto Salazar, who in turn is unlike Bob Kennedy. We have to do the most with what we have.

"They say your potential is 90 percent genetic," says Debbi Kilpatrick-Morris, winner of the 1995 U.S. National Marathon Championships. "And I believe that when you get to the elite level genetics plays a bigger role than most people realize. But I look at genetics not as a limitation but as something that shows me my possibilities. My mother was very athletic. She played many sports—tennis, softball, basketball. I think I got my athletic ability from her."

Yet while genetics is important, what we do with our talent may be even more important. The distance-running world is rife with many stories of athletes who weren't naturally gifted but succeeded in spite of that. Dan Held, a marathoner from Wisconsin, will be the first to tell you he's not exactly Carl Lewis when it comes to leg speed, but that didn't force him to throw in the towel. "Genetics will only get you to a certain point," says Held, who finished third at the 1995 U.S. Marathon Championships. "It will get you half the way—but I really do believe that the other half is plain old hard work."

Our performance potential therefore derives from our genetic makeup, which we can't change, and our training, which we do control. What we build in endurance, speed and strength will determine how well we perform—that is, run.

Aerobic Endurance: Strong on the Run

Endurance is related to the amount of energy each of us is capable of supplying to the working muscles; aerobic energy production is dependent on the amount of oxygen that can be used by the muscle. But each of us has a limit to the amount of oxygen that we can consume or utilize for energy production (maximal oxygen consumption). Maximal oxygen consumption is influenced by age, sex, genetics, body composition and, the bottom line, training.

Age: Father Time and the stopwatch. It's no secret that we slow down as we get older. But the good news is that this decline, associated with a decrease in oxygen consumption, is gradual. We don't just go from a 45-minute 10-K on Sunday to struggling up the steps on Monday. After age 25 our maximal oxygen consumption decreases about 1 percent per year. Even the best performers at the masters level, such as Nick Rose and Bob Schlau, can't match the times they ran in their thirties—they just can't consume as much oxygen for production of energy as they used to.

Sex: X versus Y. Women usually have lower oxygen consumption capacities than men. That's because women, even elite runners such as Lynn Jennings and PattiSue Plumer, have more fat stores and less muscle mass than men. Since energy metabolism takes place in the muscle, greater fat storage requires more energy to carry muscle around.

Additionally, most women consume less oxygen because of lower levels of hemoglobin (a component of red blood cells that transports oxygen to muscles), plus smaller blood volume and heart size. All of these influence the level of oxygen consumption.

Yet men and women will each improve at the same rate through training. That means if Sue runs the same workouts as Ralph—30 to 45 miles a week with repeat 400s on Monday and Thursday—she'll watch her race times drop at the same rate as Ralph's.

Body composition: muscle versus fat. Endurance is influenced by how much muscle mass and how much body fat we have. The greater the amount of muscle mass we have, the more oxygen we are capable of consuming. But we also must consider body weight. A shot-putter obviously has more muscle than a marathon runner, yet can't run as fast over 26.2 miles. That's because he weighs 50 to 100 pounds more and that extra weight burns up energy, too. When body size is considered in endurance, it is the amount of oxygen consumed per kilogram of body weight that counts.

Likewise, the greater the amount of body fat, the lower our oxygen consumption per kilogram of body weight, because energy is only produced in muscle.

Leg Speed: Hare or Tortoise?

Each of us is born with a genetically determined number of fast-contracting fibers (fast twitch) for speed and slow-contracting fibers (slow twitch) for endurance.

Fast-twitch fibers: the hare's helper. The greater the number of fast-twitch fibers we have, the faster we are able to sprint. Sprinters, such as Carl Lewis and Linford Christie, have predominantly fast-twitch fibers; they can run short distances well but cannot run long distances very effectively because they fatigue easily. As Olympic sprinter Florence Griffith Joyner found out in her disappointing attempt at a 5-K, distance training will not change fast-twitch fiber to slow-twitch fiber (Flo Jo ran a below-average time for a college runner).

At the same time, though, distance training can change some of the characteristics of fast-twitch fibers so that they're more like slow-twitch fibers. As the fiber improves its endurance capability, it loses some of its ability as a fast-twitch fiber. In other words, if you run long and slow, fast-twitch fibers get used to running long and slow and begin to mimic the slow contractions of slow-twitch fibers.

IDENTIFYING SPEED POTENTIAL

Based on your time for 100 meters, you can estimate your leg-speed potential.

RATING	TIME (SEC.)	
	Men	Women
Excellent	9.0–12.0	11.0–14.0
Very good	12.1–14.0	14.1–17.0
Average	14.1–17.0	17.1–19.0
Below average	17.1–20.0	19.1–22.0

Slow-twitch fibers: the tortoise's friend. Slow-twitch muscle fibers are more suited for the sustained energy production needed on long runs. The more slow-twitch fibers you have, the more likely you will be a distance runner. Remember the first time you went out for gym class and had to sprint around the track? The kid who finished first probably had more fast-twitch fibers, and the kid who finished last probably had more slow-twitch fibers.

Fiber-optics: Are you fast or slow? As a quick test to determine how much speed you have, simply go to the track and time yourself in an all-out run of 100 meters. If you complete the distance within three to five seconds of the existing 100-meter world record or five to ten seconds of the 200-meter record, you can be sure that you have more fast-twitch than slow-twitch fibers. The table above can be used as a rule of thumb to determine how much leg speed you have. Remember, if you don't have great leg speed, you may be more suited to running longer distances.

Strength Endurance: Training on the Run

When placed under stress, the human body adapts—it changes. The physical stress, or overload, of running causes the body to undergo several changes, such as increasing muscle, tendon and ligament strength. Hence, we get faster. However, too much stress too fast can lead to illness or injury. The body needs time and rest to adapt to training. Therefore, with careful planning, your training will build strength and speed as long as you include enough rest to avoid injury or illness.

CHAPTER

3

Going the Distance

BUILDING A BASE FOR DISTANCE RUNNING

Winter in New Hampshire is not ideal running weather. Yet Cathy O'Brien, a two-time U.S. Olympic marathoner, devotes these months to "running high mileage and lots of long runs." Why? She knows that without those long, hard months of base building in the winter, her racing in the spring and summer would suffer. "All training starts with base building," says O'Brien.

Runners aren't born—they're made. No matter how physically gifted you are, if you've only put in two weeks of training before a marathon, look out on race day! Elite runners know this well. That's why they train year-round for a peak race (such as the Boston Marathon) or season (the spring track season). And they start by building a base.

Base Building: How It Works—And Why

In the late 1950s, New Zealand distance-running coach Arthur Lydiard had his athletes cover upwards of 100 miles of slow running a week for several months prior to track season. Even milers, like Peter Snell, were out there logging 20-milers on the weekends. The long, easy distance work, Lydiard reasoned, would provide a sound foundation for more intense work later on.

Lydiard's philosophy of base building still holds up today. Without a solid winter distance base, you still might be able to race fast in the spring—at first. But not for long. Without a good base, races take more out of you, speedwork takes more recovery time, you're more apt to be injured and you just don't feel as strong.

A good case in point is U.S. Olympian Regina Jacobs. For many years she would run great races early in the season but then falter. Part of the reason was that Jacobs never spent enough time on the base-building phase of her training. Instead, she jumped quickly into speed sessions, without the strength to go with it. In 1994, however, Jacobs finally took the time to get in a good, solid base. The result? A stellar outdoor track season and a gold medal in the 1500 meters at the 1995 World Indoor Championships.

The Benefits Abound

Think of base building as the framework of your program. Base mileage builds a better circulatory system by strengthening the heart and improving circulation to the muscles.

With long, easy runs you can train your body to increase the muscles' energy production. And with less effort. This happens because blood flow is increased to the muscles as the body produces more capillaries and greater blood volume. The muscles also adapt by increasing the number of sites for energy production (mitochondria) along with increased enzymes that produce energy from fats and carbohydrates.

Other changes, such as increased ligament, tendon and muscle strength, help to protect you against injury. All these adaptations take time and patience, but they help prepare you for the speed training needed for racing.

At this time you're also building confidence. Depositing all those miles in your running bank account, to use another metaphor, will make you feel pretty secure when it's time to train faster and race. A 10-K race, for instance, won't seem so intimidating if you've regularly run ten miles in practice.

How to Build a Base

Frequency, volume, program length, and intensity. No, we're not talking about your stereo system, but the four fundamental principles of base building. Let's look at how each of these components tunes you up.

How often should I run? Keep in mind what you are trying to accomplish here: Putting miles in the bank. You don't have to run 100 miles a week, like Peter Snell, but increasing your mileage from, say, 30 to 50 miles a week will make a big difference. Therefore, the more you deposit, the more you'll be able to use later. So, we suggest running as many days as possible, at least five and preferably six, with the seventh day being a rest day or an easy run. But work up slowly and allow your body to rest. Increasing too fast is likely to lead to injury. Plan and gauge your progression; make it reasonable to fit your goals.

How many miles a week should I run? It depends. A good rule of thumb is start with your current mileage (at least 10 to 15 miles per week) and increase each week by 10 percent, throwing in an "active rest" week every two or three weeks by lowering your mileage. Jumping from 15 to 100 miles a week in three weeks invites injury.

"The trick is to start with low mileage, then gradually add more miles when you feel comfortable," says Annette Peters, 1992 U.S. Olympian at 3000 meters. "If you're not comfortable, stay at the same mileage until you do feel ready for the next step. Set a goal and build up to it gradually."

How many weeks should I devote to building a base? Depending on your goals and how much time you have to reach them, most trainers will insist that a minimum of 8 weeks should be spent on base building, more (12 to 16 weeks) if you're not in good shape when you begin.

"The number of weeks I devote to base training depends on my current fitness level," says New Zealand's Lorraine Moller, 1992 Olympic Marathon bronze medalist. "It could be as many as ten weeks." But remember, progress slowly and listen to your body to avoid overtraining. If you feel overly fatigued, take a rest day or reduce the miles. (The tables on the following pages give sample base-building schedules for beginner, intermediate and advanced levels.)

How fast should I run? All base-building miles should be run at a comfortable, conversational pace. Runners often use the "talk test" to determine if they're going too fast: If you don't have enough breath to hold a conversation with your running partner, slow down.

Generally, this means running 1 to 1½ minutes slower than your current 10-K race pace. If you run a 10-K in about 45 minutes (about 7:15 a mile), your base-building pace should be no faster than 8:15 and may be as slow as 8:45. "When you're doing your base miles," says two-time British Olympian Jill Hunter, "don't even worry about the speed."

What else should I do? During base building you might consider increasing your strength by incorporating some hill training or weight training two or three days a week. If you are running hills, go easy on the downhill to avoid heavy pounding and possible injury. Weight-training sessions should be done after your run, not before. (See chapter 4 for details on strength training.)

Getting the Most out of Your Mileage

As you are building your base mileage, concentrate on four areas: long runs, strides, racing and stretching. Sure, you can disregard these elements and still get in shape, but your gains will not be as plentiful.

SAMPLE BASE-BUILDING SCHEDULE: BEGINNER

A beginner is someone already running at least 20 miles a week.

WEEK	WEEKLY TOTAL (MI.)	DAILY MILEAGE
1	23	5, 4, rest, 5, rest, 5, 4
2	25	5, 5, rest, 5, rest, 5, 5
3	23	4, 5, rest, 5, rest, 5, 4
4	27	6, 5, rest, 6, 5, 5, rest
5	29	6, 4, 5, rest, 5, 4, 5
6	25	5, 4, 4, 6, 4, 4, rest
7	31	7, 5, 4, rest, 5, 5, 5
8	33	7, 6, 5, rest, 6, 5, 4

Long runs. Olympian Jeff Galloway calls the long run "the single most important element in your training program." The long run teaches your body to burn more fat as fuel, thus training it for endurance. It builds stamina and confidence, and gives you something to look forward to the other days of the week.

Rather than adding mileage to two or three different runs during the week, though, as novice runners tend to do, you should add miles to just *one* run a week.

In terms of duration, the long run is your only hard workout each week, though it won't seem hard because you're still running at a conversational pace. How far you eventually want to go is up to you. If you're training for 5-Ks and 10-Ks, you might want to top off at 10 to 12 miles. If your goal is a marathon, work up to long runs of 15 to 20 miles.

Strides. Twice a week, run four to eight pickups of about 100 to 200 yards, with a short rest in between. Strides help increase leg turnover, not necessarily speed, so the pace should be quick but not all-out—about one-mile-race tempo. Concentrate on smooth running form. "During base building I still do 8 × 100 meters twice a week so I don't lose the feeling of getting up on my toes and going fast," says Laurie Gomez-Henes, a member of the 1995 U.S. World Track and Field Championships team at 10,000 meters.

Racing. If you're bored with your training, use a race as a workout, preferably during a rest week when you're dropping back your mileage and cutting out your long run. Race for enjoyment, and think of it as just another training day.

Racing is not usually done during base building, so keep the distance manageable (a 5-K or a 10-K) and the pace moderate (faster than your current training pace but slower than your racing pace). This will refresh your legs and may even get the competitive juices flowing.

On the other hand, don't force yourself to race if you don't feel like it. "I prefer to race as little as possible during my base-building phase," says Steve Holman, a 1992 U.S. Olympian at 1500 meters. "It's my time off from racing and I use it for mental relaxation."

Stretching. During the base-building phase, slower running (shorter strides) lessens your legs' range of motion. Over time, slower daily runs can tighten your ligaments and muscles. Stretch before and after each run to maintain flexibility. (For a complete discussion of stretching, see chapter 9.)

Consistency Counts

One of the biggest challenges Debbi Kilpatrick-Morris, winner of the 1995 U.S. National Marathon Championships, has to face each year

---

SAMPLE BASE-BUILDING SCHEDULE: INTERMEDIATE

The intermediate runner is serious about running and has been consistently running about 35 miles a week.

WEEK	WEEKLY TOTAL (MI.)	DAILY MILEAGE
1	38	7, 5, 6, rest, 7, 5, 8
2	40	6, 7, 6, rest, 7, 5, 9
3	38	5, 6, 7, rest, 8, 5, 7
4	43	6, 8, 6, rest, 7, 6, 10
5	46	6, 8, 7, rest, 8, 7, 10
6	40	6, 7, 6, rest, 8, 7, 6
7	48	6, 7, 6, 4, 8, 6, 11
8	50	5, 8, 6, 5, 8, 6, 12

is to keep from doing too much too soon in her marathon buildup. "The temptation is always there to jump up the mileage dramatically," says Kilpatrick-Morris. "There's always that desire to do more than you're really ready for. But that can backfire."

As you increase your weekly mileage and gain confidence, you might be tempted, like Kilpatrick-Morris, to speed up the process by making gargantuan leaps in your mileage.

Don't.

The running world is littered with athletes who've tried to do too much too soon and ended up sick or injured. It's much better to spend 8 to 12 weeks building from 40 to 60 miles a week than it is to jump up too fast in 1 or 2 weeks—and then lie in bed with an injury or the flu. Overtraining can wear down your resistance (immunity) to colds, flu and other infections.

"A steady progression of mileage is the key," says 1985 Boston Marathon champ Lisa Weidenbach, "but it's hard to do." By nature, runners are not patient. We want to up our mileage as quickly as possible. We want to get the drudgery of slow training out of the way so we can get to the fun and challenging stuff—the speedwork and the racing. But like it or not, if you want to run well in the summer, you'll have to spend most of winter and spring diligently building a base. You can't get base building out of the way in three weeks.

SAMPLE BASE-BUILDING SCHEDULE: ADVANCED

An advanced runner usually trains seven days a week and has consistently run 45 to 50 miles a week.

WEEK	WEEKLY TOTAL (MI.)	DAILY MILEAGE
1	48	6, 6, 8, 6, 6, 6, 10
2	51	6, 6, 9, 6, 6, 6, 12
3	48	6, 6, 9, 6, 7, 6, 8
4	54	7, 6, 9, 6, 7, 6, 13
5	57	6, 7, 10, 6, 7, 7, 14
6	50	6, 7, 9, 6, 7, 6, 9
7	60	7, 7, 10, 7, 7, 7, 15
8	64	7, 8, 11, 7, 8, 7, 16

TIPS FROM THE TOP

BUILDING A BASE

A strong running base lays the foundation for success, as each of these elite runners can attest.

Budd Coates, three-time U.S. Olympic Marathon Trials qualifier (1984, 1988 and 1992): "Begin base training with no quality (faster workouts) in mind, and only run quality if adaptation to mileage is going perfectly."

Lynn Jennings, 1992 Olympic 10,000 meters bronze medalist: "During base building I maintain my speed by running fartlek, tempo runs and some hillwork. Not everything is easy running, that's for sure, but I do not go to the track."

Bob Kennedy, 1992 U.S. Olympian at 5000 meters: "My base is about two to three months of relatively high mileage, ending four or five months before my peak month. But just because it's high mileage doesn't mean it's all slow. I'll do some hills, tempo runs and strides, but no serious track work."

Reuben Reina, 1992 U.S. Olympian at 5000 meters: "I do the bulk of my base training in the fall in preparation for the spring track season, where faster intervals start coming into the training."

Steve Spence, 1991 World Marathon Championships bronze medalist and a 1992 Olympic Marathoner: "Base building takes time. Take a good eight to ten weeks to build a solid base without interrupting your training."

By keeping to a slow and steady course, you'll worry less about an off week every now and then. Instead of getting in the 50 miles you planned, for instance, say you end up with 42. The trick is to look at the big picture and know it will even out. "On a buildup to a marathon I start with 12 to 16 weeks of solid base training," says 1992 British Olympic marathoner Steve Brace. "And my emphasis is on consistency throughout those weeks, rather than on good and bad weeks."

So how do you get through good and bad weeks during those long, slow months? All runners have their own tricks, but three strategies have proved effective.

1. Vary the terrain on which you run. After three days on an asphalt road, for example, you might want to switch to a dirt road, a park trail or a golf course.
2. Change your routes. If you often start from home, run your routes in reverse occasionally. Experiment with new park trails or go cross-country through fields and forests.
3. Run with friends. The miles pass more quickly when you have someone to talk to—and someone to share your running dreams. "Run with people who are trying to reach the same goal, or with someone who is training for the same race," says 2:11 marathoner Don Janicki.

Use these tricks, and the base-building phase will not only go by faster, it may even be enjoyable. And that's the real trick of any long training program.

Strength Training

RUNNING HILLS AND PUMPING IRON

The popularly held image of the distance runner as scarecrow-thin is about as dated as the hula hoop. Take a close look at elite distance runners today, like Todd Williams and Anne Marie Lauck, and you'll see that while there isn't any excess baggage, they aren't exactly Ichabod Cranes and Olive Oyls. From their calf muscles to their shoulders and arms, many elite runners are well-developed and very strong for their size.

The Strong Survive

What has brought about this change? For one thing, strength training can help you with your kick. The stronger your legs—and upper body—toward the end of a race, the faster you will be able to sprint. "Speed in distance races depends more on strength than on raw speed," explains Bob Kennedy, a 1992 U.S. Olympian at 5000 meters.

For another thing, strength training helps to balance out the body. A strong—but not bulky—upper body serves as a counterweight to the well-developed legs of a runner. And that upper body can come into play on turns and downhills, and in the mass confusion of big-time road races.

Perhaps the greatest benefit of strength training is that it helps to prevent injuries. Stronger hamstrings and quadriceps, for instance, stablize the knee and can ward off one of the most common running injuries—runner's knee.

Runners can use two approaches to build strength: one old (hill running) and one relatively new (weight training). Both build muscle and endurance by working against resistance, either by working your body against gravity or by lifting weights. Each approach plays a role in a runner's fitness and health.

TIPS FROM THE TOP

STRENGTH TRAINING

Resistance training is important for most elite runners, who often incorporate both hills and weight training to support their running. It must work, because their times show the results. These top runners share their most successful secrets.

Steve Brace, 1992 British Olympic marathoner: "Not all courses are flat; therefore a person who doesn't do hillwork will be disadvantaged. Do your hill efforts by the watch. For example, three minutes hard, then three minutes easy on a hilly run to simulate racing. Also, I like to do short hill repeats—one to two minutes—jogging back down to recover before I begin another."

Laurie Gomez-Henes, member of the 1995 U.S. World Track and Field Championships team at 10,000 meters: "I do a four-week hill phase near the end of the base period in cross-country. The hills I run are 200- to 800-meters long. The long hills are for strength; the shorter ones are a great help with knee lift."

Don Janicki, 2:11 marathoner: "I do a lot of distance runs over hills, but do not do hill repeats. I weight train three days a week. During my base training I do three sets of 10 reps for my heavy lifting; in the competitive season I do two sets of 15 reps with lighter weights."

Anne Marie Lauck, member of the 1995 U.S. World Track and Field Championships team at 10,000 meters: "I don't do specific hill training, as the terrain where I live is very rolling and hilly. When I do fartlek workouts, I get in my good hillwork. I also use free weights for upper body strength. I do three sets of 15 for biceps, triceps, bench press, lats and shoulder shrugs."

Head for the Hills

The Australians did it in the 1950s; the Kenyans do it today. We're talking about running hills. Those lean-into-it, quad-burning, run-over-the-top-with-my-pulse-pounding-in-my-head-like-a-gong hills. There's no other workout quite like a hill session, and, according to two-time U.S. Olympic Marathon Trials qualifier Jon Sinclair, "Running hills is an absolute necessity for a road racer." Hill running amplifies aerobic benefit, leg strength and power, and endurance—

Jerry Lawson, 2:10 marathoner: "My strength is my strength training. Twice a week I do endurance lifting—high repetitions on every machine on the circuit. I feel really fit, and it helps me mentally. In races I know I have the strength to carry on."

Cathy O'Brien, two-time U.S. Olympic marathoner (1988 and 1992): "Hill training is beneficial for building strength and useful for road racing, which may involve hilly courses. I don't do specific hill repeats, but the area I live and train in is very hilly so my daily runs have rolling hills throughout."

PattiSue Plumer, two-time Olympian (1988 at 3000 meters, 1992 at 3000 meters and 1500 meters): "I like running on trails, and the trails I run have hills. Also, I find it breaks the monotony of my training. I think that you can get cardiovascular work without great wear and tear on the legs if you run easy downhill. I also weight train four days a week for 20 minutes each session: two days working on my upper body and two days on lower."

Ric Sayre, 1983 Los Angeles Marathon winner and elite masters runner: "I have always used hills to supplement the limited speed-work I do. A typical 12- to 13-mile run will include a 1000-foot climb in elevation. I also lift weights once or twice a week. Each session is only 15 to 20 minutes—nothing major—but it helps."

Lisa Weidenbach, 1985 Boston Marathon champ: "I do hills during the beginning of my marathon training, and that eventually helps lead me into track workouts. I also lift weights two times a week, but upper body only! I do eight exercises, concentrating on lats, biceps, triceps, deltoids, chest, back and stomach."

all the important factors that make for great running.

But before you head out the door and up the nearest incline, let's consider what hills can do for you and how to run them. Then we'll talk about different workouts and when to run hills.

What Hills Can Do for You

Heartbreak Hill in the Boston Marathon. Cardiac Hill in the Pittsburgh Marathon. Names like these suggest that hills are dangerous—to be feared because of the pain or damage they can inflict. They're to be dreaded, like extra push-ups when we screwed up in gym class or baseball practice. ("No! You've messed up again! Go give me ten hills ...now!")

But elite runners are far past their initial fear of hills, for they know them to be one of the most beneficial training tools around. Hills give us strength and endurance, and even help improve our running form.

Hills build stronger legs and lungs. Hillwork will strengthen your quadriceps, hamstrings and calf muscles much more quickly and efficiently than running on the flat. Research has shown that improvement in performance through increased muscle strength is best achieved with movements as close as possible to the activity. Therefore, uphill running should make you a stronger runner than if you lifted weights.

Aerobically, you condition yourself to have greater endurance when you run uphill because you work much harder over the distance than if you were running on level ground. This translates into better endurance in your other training runs and in racing.

Hills clean up your form. Repeated hillwork will help clean up your form because any wasted or inefficient motion is magnified tenfold going up a hill. If, for example, you tend to lean too much to one side on each foot plant, you'll feel this going up a hill, and by the third or fourth repeat you'll be consciously trying to fix it—because it is keeping you from getting to the top of the hill quickly.

Another benefit to your form is increased emphasis on knee lift. If you have a shuffle, hills will force you to raise those knees and, if kept up, eventually improve your flat-road stride. This is especially important in older runners whose strides tend to shorten and flatten out with age.

How to Run Hills

Running hills is not the same as running on the flat, so when you decide to do hillwork, concentrate on these tips.

Never start cold. The bottom of a hill is not the place to begin your workout. Always jog *into* the hill, gradually picking up your pace on the flat until you've reached *hill-repeat* pace at the bottom. Then start up.

Maintain effort. You won't be going as fast up the hill as you were on the flat, but keep the effort level high. How hard are you breathing? How fast is your heart pumping? How much of a burning sensation is in your legs? Monitor these things on your way up. Think of going up a hill in a car: You change gears and slow down, but the car's engine works just as hard.

Maintain form. Lean into the hill, shorten your stride and concentrate on knee lift. Pump your arms—not excessively, but use them to help propel you to the top.

Run through the hill. In other words, when you reach the top, don't stop. As you crest, you'll feel the workload drop; use the extra energy to run through the crown at high effort for several strides. Then go into your recovery jog.

Go down easy. Be careful running down hills because of the increased pounding to your legs and feet. Running repeats during hill training should be spaced with easy downhill jogs to avoid injury.

Hill Workouts

Running uphill is hard work. Perhaps no other workout comes closer to the actual muscle fatigue you get from racing. Therefore it's best to run hills only once a week, or at the most twice. Any more and you will be constantly tearing down muscle fiber—and not taking the time to rebuild. That can lead to injury.

Depending on whether endurance, speed or strength is the focus, elite runners use three types of hill workouts: long hill repeats, short hill repeats and hill runs. Steve Spence, 1991 World Marathon Championships bronze medalist and a 1992 Olympic marathoner, uses all three.

Long hills. For endurance, Spence will find a long (½-mile to 2-mile) hill at a moderate grade and run four to eight repeats, concentrating on maintaining an even rhythm and keeping his form clean. This isn't speedwork, but he runs the hills at close to his 10-K race effort, with little recovery before the next repeat.

Short hills. For speed, Spence will find a shorter (200- to 600-yard) hill at a steeper grade (say 5 to 6 percent) and run 8 to 16 repeats, concentrating on power and really blasting up the hill. Recovery should be longer than for long hills, with an easy downhill jog.

Hill runs. For strength, Spence will run an hour or two on a hilly path in the mountains, concentrating on maintaining an even effort, up and down, throughout the entire run.

When to Run Hills

Think of hillwork and the effort involved like your long training runs before a marathon: Your body needs time to recover before you race. Because they are extremely hard work, run hills in the preparatory phase of training, before your racing phase; if you keep hills in

---

TREADMILLS AND OTHER HILL ALTERNATIVES

Most of us can easily find a 10- to 15-percent-grade hill to charge up every now and then. But a few of us, like Houston's Joy Smith, a 2:34 marathoner, have to drive three hours to find a hill made by Mother Nature. Yet that doesn't mean that Smith doesn't run hills.

She does her hillwork on a treadmill, setting the grade to mimic particular grades of hills at upcoming races. For example, in the months before the 1993 Boston Marathon, Smith ran hill workouts on a treadmill that copied the series of famous hills at Boston that culminates with Heartbreak Hill; come race day, she was as ready for those hills as a Boston native. She finished ninth with 2:38:35.

Other options include charging up stadium steps or the numerous stair-climbing machines in health clubs. If stairs are used in place of hills, be careful coming down the steps—this places a lot of stress on the feet and ankles.

---

your schedule, skip them in the few weeks before a big race and you can't go wrong.

Steve Spence uses hills during his base-building phase as "bridge work," transitional runs that help his body go from the endurance phase (base miles) to speed sessions on the track. For Spence, "Hills toughen my body, get it used to faster paced work to come. If I jump right into 400-meter repeats after base work, I'll be setting myself up for injury and breakdown."

Hit the Weights

Years ago, the only time elite runners saw the weight room was when they were passing by on the way to the showers. Inside were a breed of athletes they abhorred—no-neck, thickly muscled guys who believed bigger was better. If elite runners entered that room, they were not only wasting time with exercises that seemed to offer no benefit to their 10-K times, but they also felt conspicuously out of place amid all that bulk.

That stigma has taken a long time to overcome. Indeed, some running books written just ten years ago stated that weight training had no benefit at all for distance runners; others recommended lifting portable typewriters for an upper body workout!

Times have changed. Spence, for instance, sometimes hits the weight room three times a week; two-time British Olympian Jill Hunter lifts four times a week. In fact, almost every elite runner today incorporates some sort of weight training (Nautilus, free weights or hand weights) into their weekly schedule.

The Physiology of Resistance Training

In order to fully benefit from your weight training, you need to train smart and be aware of what each type of workout can do for you. Just like for running the 100 meters or a marathon, specificity of training applies to resistance training.

Lifting heavy weights for a low number of reps is more specific for fast-twitch muscle fibers used in sprinting; lifting lighter weights for a high number of reps is more specific for slow-twitch fibers and may help strength endurance during a kick at the end of a race.

WHY—AND HOW—STEVE SPENCE WORKS WITH WEIGHTS

At five feet nine inches and 135 pounds, Steve Spence will never be mistaken for an American Gladiator. He's best known for taking the bronze for the marathon at the 1991 World Championships. But take a closer look at his physique and you'll find that there's a lot of muscle on his lean runner's frame. "Depending on my phase of training, I'll lift weights one or as many as three times a week," says Spence.

Under the tutelage of strength coach Doug Lenz, who also works with NBA and NFL players, Spence lifts to improve strength and endurance in all parts of his body—including legs, once thought a taboo area for runners because of increasing bulk.

In the base-building phase, the intensity is high (two to three sets with heavy weights). As racing season nears, Spence cuts back on both the weight and the number of sets to keep his muscles fresh for hard track workouts and, eventually, peak races. "As a rule, the greater the intensity of my running, the less intense my weight training," Spence says.

And that makes sense, because intense weight training stresses the fast-twitch muscle fibers, the same ones used for speed workouts. Cutting back on the heavy weights helps avoid overtired muscles.

The controversy surrounding the use of weight training to increase distance running performance is ongoing. If weight training is
to be a part of your program, it is probably most useful during your
preseason training and should never be used as a substitute for running. Even if the benefits of weight training for distance runners are
minimal, however, it does strengthen the support structures of joints
and could help in preventing injuries.

Lifting may be more beneficial for shorter races than for distance
running, as its benefits for improving maximal oxygen consumption
are still in question.

Form over Substance: The Key to Results

Good form is essential to getting the most out of your lifting, just
as it is with running.

Control the movement. Jerking, or throwing the barbell up in a
bench press, for example, might impress others in the gym (especially if you grunt loud enough) but it won't work the muscles the
way a smooth, controlled lift does.

Control is the key here. Work muscles through the full range of
the joint, and don't strain or change the angle of pull.

Remember that timing is everything. Use even, steady movements to lift and lower weights. A good rule of thumb is to lift on a
count of two and lower for a count of four. Use more control when
releasing the weight because this negative movement also builds
strength.

Breathe with the movement. Breathing is important to ensure
blood flow back to the heart, preventing big fluctuations in blood
pressure. Exhale on the lift, and inhale as you lower the weight.

Free Weights or Machines?

The debate over which weight training system is better—free
weights or machines—has been raging since Nautilus machines were
first introduced in the 1970s.

There are advantages to both.

With free weights you get a more *balanced* workout, because
when you do a set of arm curls with a dumbbell, for instance, you're
also working other muscle groups in the area. When you use pulley,
cable or pneumatic weight machines, however, you work only the
muscle group you want to train—so you get a more *precise* workout.
Using an arm-curl machine, for example, will target only the biceps
and forearms.

If you're inexperienced, machines can be faster than free weights—

TYPICAL TRAINING SCHEDULE FOR LAURIE GOMEZ-HENES

North Carolina State's multiple all-American Laurie Gomez-Henes is one of the bright stars in the future of U.S. distance running. Gomez-Henes also supplements her training with twice-weekly weight sessions. "I'll do the circuit," she says. "Light weights, high repetitions. It *does* help make me a better runner because I'm stronger all over." Here's how Gomez-Henes fits her weight workouts into a typical training week. Note that she lifts after an easy workout.

Sunday		3–4 mi., easy (6:40 pace)
Monday	A.M.	3 mi., easy
	P.M.	2 mi. warm-up and cooldown
		3–4 repeat mi. (4:55–5:05 pace)
		2 min. recovery jog between each
Tuesday	A.M.	3 mi., easy
	P.M.	6 mi.; form drills and *weights*
Wednesday	P.M.	8 mi., moderate (6:15 pace)
Thursday	P.M.	2 mi. warm-up and cooldown
		3 sets of 4 × 400 m. (70 sec.)
		100 m. jog between each, 2 min. rest between sets
Friday	A.M.	3 mi., easy
	P.M.	6 mi., easy; form drills and *weights*
Saturday	A.M.	10 mi., easy

just insert a pin or push a button and the weight is set; no need to mess with heavy plates. Plus, you don't need a spotter for the bench press.

Free weighters will counter that working out with a partner is the best way to stay focused and improve. And the debate goes on.

From a runner's standpoint, where lifting is a supplemental exercise, it's probably best to use what is most convenient and takes the least amount of time. For most runners, that means machines. But for more experienced lifters, who usually have their own weights at home or a regular training partner at the gym, free weights may be the answer.

Don't Weigh Me Down

You'll notice that elite runners who lift regularly don't have the bulging muscles of big-time body builders—and there's a reason. The majority of runners, like Jill Hunter, lift light weights at a high number of repetitions (two or three sets of 12) to build strong, sleek, endurance muscles, not the Popeye forearms that come from lifting heavier weights at a low number of reps.

The proof? No Olympic gold medalist from the 1500 meters on up has had biceps that belong in an arm wrestling match.

That's because they didn't need them.

5

Speed Training

LEARNING TO RUN FASTER

You've put in a good base. You've gained additional strength from hill running and weight lifting. But if you want to improve your times this year, the best way to do it is to run fast in practice.

It's called specificity of training. Simply put, it means that to perform a certain task, say shooting free throws or running a fast 5-K, you must practice the moves and skills of that task specifically. "To race fast, one must train fast," says 1992 Olympic 10,000 meters bronze medalist Lynn Jennings.

And that means speed training.

What Is Speed Training?

For many runners, the very phrase *speed training* hurts. It conjures up images of bending double at the waist, gasping for breath after a hard effort. Yet this is not necessarily so. A well-thought-out speed-training plan will take you to faster times in races without leaving you crawling off the track.

You learn to run faster the same way you learned to run in the first place—a little at a time. Do you want to lower your race pace from 6:20 per mile to 6:00? Then you have to start practicing to run at that pace—first for a short distance, then to sustain it.

In speed training, you run a set fast pace (like 6:00 per mile) over a measured distance (like 400 meters, or a quarter-mile) repeatedly, with recovery phases in between. So if your goal is a 6:00 pace, plan to run these quarter-miles in 90 seconds. Because distances are easily gauged on a track, that's the ideal place for speedwork, but measured sections of a road or trail are okay, too.

Remember to set realistic goals and to progress slowly to avoid injury. Just as you wouldn't expect to jump from 50 to 100 miles a

TIPS FROM THE TOP

SPEEDWORK

Steve Brace, 1992 British Olympic marathoner: "Short recovery is what's required for distance runners. Usually recovery time is half the effort time, i.e., 5 minutes effort and a 2½-minute recovery. And there is no need for flat-out efforts, only a pace that is about race pace."

Budd Coates, three-time U.S. Olympic Marathon Trials qualifier (1984, 1988 and 1992): "Concentrate on good form and make sure the speedwork pace is related to present fitness levels. Don't overestimate your abilities and don't try to run too fast too soon."

Steve Holman, 1992 U.S. Olympian at 1500 meters: "Put off speed training in your program as long as possible, because once you start speed training there isn't anything else you can do to improve speed. Work on strength building as long as possible."

Jill Hunter, two-time British Olympian (3000 meters in 1988 and 10,000 meters in 1992): "Speed training means hard training. It's tough, but the perseverance is worth it. Your times will come down."

Lynn Jennings, 1992 Olympic 10,000 meters bronze medalist: "Don't be afraid to work hard on the track. Track workouts are the backbone of a good performance."

Bob Kennedy, 1992 U.S. Olympian at 5000 meters: "Speed in distance races has little to do with raw speed and a lot to do with strength. Your innate speed doesn't help at the end of a race if you don't have the strength from your base training."

Annette Peters, 1992 U.S. Olympian at 3000 meters: "Make sure you have a good base—and a little speed, too—before starting any speed-training program. I always do 150s or 200s after a workout, even during the base-building phase, but they aren't in spikes or timed during the base-building phase."

Reuben Reina, 1992 U.S. Olympian at 5000 meters: Don't rush into speed training. Gradually start to incorporate your intervals by using slower, controlled workouts. This prepares your body for the added stress you'll be putting on it later.

week in your base-building phase, you won't go to the track and hammer 80-second quarters till you drop if your best all-out quarter is 78 seconds.

What Speedwork Does for You

You've put in a good base, and you're stronger from hill running and weight lifting. As the next step, speed training builds on your base training and is more specific to racing. By increasing your ability to run faster over a long distance, speedwork takes you to faster race times.

Training specificity is important in developing the energy system that is primarily used during racing. Recall that long, slow running uses mainly the slow-twitch muscle fibers and the aerobic, or oxygen burning, system for energy production. For shorter, more intense distances, say 800 meters, the anaerobic (without oxygen) energy system becomes the predominant supply of energy. So speed training teaches the body to run anaerobically; that is, to run fast when there's a lack of oxygen going to the working muscles.

By training more intensely, you learn to deal with lactic acid buildup in your legs—that heavy feeling that comes on late in races. A by-product of anaerobic metabolism, lactic acid can alter your stride. Consequently, by conditioning the body to run faster, you are training the anaerobic system that is important during shorter races.

Finally, you are training the fast-twitch muscle fibers needed to produce leg speed.

Speedwork How-Tos

Regardless of your individual workout, speedwork consists of at least four elements, all of which vary according to your goals and abilities.

1. *How far?* The distance you want to repeat could be anywhere from 100 meters to two or three miles, but usually it's less than a mile—and it's definitely shorter than your racing distance. Some coaches suggest keeping the time to 90 seconds, which will dictate your longest target distance.
2. *How much rest?* The rest period before you run another repeat can be long (complete rest) or short (30 seconds), casual (jogging a lap) or strict (two minutes by the stopwatch). It may be determined by your pulse rate or simply by a perceived sense of relief, depending on the type of speed workout you're doing.

CAVEAT SPEEDSTER

For all the good it does, speed training is also risky—increasing the chance of injuries. So before you step on the gas, heed the following advice.

1. *Skip the first year.* If you've just begun a running program, take the time to build your endurance and leg strength first. Have at least a year's worth of running in the bank before you hit the track. "Make sure you have a solid distance base before starting any speed training," says Annette Peters, 1992 U.S. Olympian at 3000 meters.
2. *Move up gradually.* Shift into the fast lane with what 1992 Olympic marathoner Steve Spence calls "transitional workouts," such as road fartlek and hills. "They bridge the gap between long, slow runs and fast track sessions."
3. *Have a plan.* Map out your speed-training program like you would your base-building phase. Know what you want to accomplish by the end of the eight weeks and then go for it.
4. *Be patient.* Don't expect to improve each session. Some runners time themselves the first week of speed training, then hide the watch until four or five weeks later. "It's not the stellar workouts that get you in shape, but consistent speed training," says Janis Klecker, 1992 U.S. Olympic marathoner.
5. *Don't overdo it.* Ten quarters in 90 seconds might be a good workout, but it doesn't necessarily follow that 20 repeats in 90 seconds would be better—if it leads to injury or illness. "I always hold back a little on my speed sessions," says Lorraine Moller, the 1992 Olympic Marathon bronze medalist. "I find I get better returns. The 100-percent-eyeballs-out efforts I save for races."
6. *Get ready to run.* Jumping into a speed session without warming up is an invitation to a muscle pull or ligament damage.
7. *Cool down, too.* A slow jog or post-run stretch will help flush out the lactic acid in your legs and help alleviate those dead legs the day after speed sessions.

3. *How hard?* Your intensity, or pace, ranges from hard to easy. Hard workouts will be run at under race pace, say 85 seconds per 400 meters for an 18:38 5-Ker (someone who averages 90 seconds a lap during a 5-K). Easier workouts

will be slower than race pace, 95 seconds per 400 meters for an 18:38 5-Ker.

4. *How many?* The number of times you cover the distance is directly related to the other three variables. As those factors are pushed up, repetitions will drop. If you cut back on distance or intensity, you'll want to do more repeats to ensure a strong workout.

Intervals: Getting Ready to Race

Considered by many to be the most effective form of speed training, intervals are the backbone of most elite athletes' race preparation. All speedwork involves some variation of interval training, but not all speedwork is so precise. That's why interval workouts are best run on the track, where exact distance, pace and recovery can be monitored.

Sample interval workouts include everything from 100-meter sprints to 800-meter or mile repeats. The plan is to run the efforts faster than race pace, and to monitor the rest in between. In fact, the word *interval* refers to the rest period between each repeat, not the hard 100 or 400 meters you run.

The key to interval training is the ratio between the running segment (measured in time or distance) and the rest interval between each effort. A harder work effort means a longer rest period before the next repeat. Suppose you are running repeat 400 meters on the track in 70 seconds. If your rest period is also 400 meters or 70 seconds, this ratio is 1:1. Obviously, the lower the ratio, the closer to race conditions you get. Once you determine your ratio, don't change it just because you are tired toward the last interval—be consistent.

Intervals not only get you ready to race, they tell you what you can expect in your race. Suppose you're aiming to hold a 6:00 pace in your next 5-K. If running 6 × 400 meters in 88 seconds (just under your race-pace goal) with a one-minute rest is still too hard ten days before your race, you might want to readjust your goal. On the other hand, if you crank out those 400s in 81 to 83 seconds, you might want to shoot for a faster pace come race day.

Like other parts of your training, remember to vary your interval workouts. Running 8 × 400 meters every week will grow stale fast. Elite athletes like to mix it up, running 400s one week, 200s the next and maybe 300s the following week. Or they'll run 200s, 400s and 800s all in one workout. They also run ladder drills, starting with, say, 1600, then going down the ladder: 1200, 800, 400, 200.

What happens when running 8 × 400 meters in 85 seconds becomes too easy, compared with six weeks ago when you started interval training? When you reach a plateau in your interval workout, you have three ways to go.

1. Maintain your pace but add repetitions, perhaps increasing to 10 or 12.
2. Drop the number of repetitions and pick up the speed, say running 6 × 400 in 82 seconds.
3. Keep the same workout but cut the rest interval between each effort.

Since intervals are supposed to be fast, why not invite some friends to the track to run with you? Running with someone will make the workouts go faster and your hard efforts seem easier—as long as the thrill of competition doesn't get out of hand. Remember: You're running against the clock (trying to hit 85 for the 400), not your training partner.

Lisa Weidenbach, 1985 Boston Marathon champion, even uses intervals when training for a marathon—such as 5 × 1 mile 40 to 45 seconds faster than race pace with a 90-second recovery. "I like the short recovery between miles," she says, "rather than two to three minutes. I do end up running the miles about five seconds slower, but who cares? The short recovery makes me stronger."

Repetitions: Early Season Workouts

For our purposes, repetitions, or reps, will refer to longer speed workouts (800 meters to two miles) run at slower than race pace, with a long rest in between. Repetitions are early season workouts. A typical repetition workout for an 18:38 5-K runner (6:00 a mile) would be 3 × 1 mile in 6:15 to 6:30, with a half-mile jog between each rep. Or it could be 6 × 800 meters in three minutes, with a 400-meter jog between each rep.

Unlike intervals, repetitions can be run on or off the track, as long as you measure the distance accurately. Some runners prefer to run them off the track because it's easier on the legs (less force on the knees and hips from the turns), not to mention the mind (no one likes running in circles for weeks on end).

Fartlek: Less Structured Change of Pace

Watch any group of kids during grade-school recess and you'll see a modified fartlek, or speed play, workout going on: They'll jog

TWO VERSIONS OF FARTLEK WORKOUTS

Nowadays most fartlek workouts are run with either the clock or the course as a guide. These two sample workouts show each kind.

Running fartlek by the clock: Jog for ten minutes on a trail to warm up. Next, run five minutes at roughly 5-K race pace, then slow to a jog for two minutes before running one minute at mile race pace, slowing into three minutes at 5-K race pace, followed by five minutes of jogging, followed by ten minutes at 10-K race pace and then ten minutes of jogging.

Following a fartlek course: Warm up for ten minutes on a trail you are familiar with. Now, run the flat section (roughly a mile) at 5-K race pace, slow to a jog as you approach the steep hill, sprint it for all it's worth to the top, jog to catch your breath as the trail opens up to a field, pick it up to 10-K race pace once around the field (about 1½ miles), then jog back down the hill before running to the first bridge on the way back at mile race pace (about 600 yards), then jog in (recovery).

for a while, sprint, then jog some more, pick it up to the backstop and then sprint to the jungle gym. Without knowing it, they're getting in a great workout—and that's the key to fartlek. It keeps the mind fresh while the body still does hard work.

To run pure fartlek, it helps to have the mind of a poet and the body of a gazelle. Compared with other speedwork, fartlek is far less structured: The distances may vary and the rest interval is usually a slow jog. The pace also changes from easy to hard efforts over a given distance. You run as the body feels, charging across a field, slowing to a jog to cross a bridge, then picking up the pace on a wood-chip path.

In mimicking gazelles, most of us, including elite runners, can use fartlek running as a chance to improve while improvising, ranging from a free-spirited run to something more regimented, based on time segments or distances (see "Two Versions of Fartlek Workouts").

Time Trials: A Race Preview

More than any other kind of speedwork, the time trial predicts race performance. By timing themselves over a certain segment of

TYPICAL TRAINING SCHEDULE FOR ANNETTE PETERS

Oregon's Annette Peters, of Eugene, shocked the U.S. track world when she doubled—winning both the 1500 and 3000 meters at the 1991 U.S. Championships. Yet it should come as no surprise, once you look at her speed workouts. Peters runs three speed sessions a week, mixing together short and long intervals and a modified time trial on Saturday.

Sunday	8 mi., 7:00 pace
Monday	7 mi., 7:00 pace
Tuesday	Track workout:
	2 mi. warm-up and cooldown
	3 × 800 m. (2:23), 400 m. jog/walk recovery
	3 × 400 m. (:68), 400 m. jog/walk recovery
	3 × 200 m. (:32), 200 m. jog/walk recovery
Wednesday	7 mi., 7:00 pace
Thursday	Track workout:
	2 mi. warm-up and cooldown
	3 × 1 mi. (5:30 pace)
	4 × 150 m. alternate float (quick) and fast (sprint)
Friday	6 mi., 7:00 pace
Saturday	Track workout:
	2 mi. warm-up and cooldown
	Hard 600 m., then 400 m. rest
	Hard 400 m., then 600 m. rest
	Hard 300 m.

their upcoming race, runners can judge how well they can hold pace for an extended period of time.

A time trial for an upcoming 5-K might be a two-mile run at a predicted 5-K pace. Your performance in this partial-race simulation will give you a good idea of your race readiness. Time trials will give you confidence by showing what you can accomplish, based on your training.

Many elites will use races as time trials to judge pace as well as overall fitness. In 1991, for example, two weeks before their victories in the New York City Marathon, both Salvador Garcia and Liz McColgan ran the Youngstown International Peace Race 10-K. McColgan won the women's division, while Garcia finished a close second to Keith Brantly. Both performances hinted at a high fitness level and mental readiness, which, in turn, was borne out on the streets of New York 14 days later.

Indeed, 1983 Los Angeles Marathon winner and elite masters runner Ric Sayre rarely does any speedwork other than races. "I don't do much speed training," he says, "but I use weekly races, say 10-Ks, for speed training leading up to a marathon."

CHAPTER
6

Training Logs

A Piece of Your History

Writers keep journals. Artists keep sketchbooks. Runners keep training logs.

More than your trophy case or your T-shirt collection, your training log is your running career, from *A* to *Z*. And it is something you can be proud of. Like a diary, it is a piece of you put down for posterity.

Many runners have turned their training logs into mini-diaries, detailing not only the day's run but also their other activities that day ("went to the mall with Suzy"), moods ("depressed over a problem at work") and even daydreams ("I wish I was in Hawaii right now; I hate running in the snow!"). And while these more personal records help you see into your mind as well as your body, for our purposes here we'll concentrate on a training log that's focused on your daily workouts. Most serious runners keep simple, run-oriented training logs.

What a Training Log Can Do for You

A training log is a useful tool for runners at every level. Beginners can watch their progress, and writing daily entries reinforces their commitment to fitness. Intermediates get a lift from seeing improvement and can use the log to set new goals. And advanced runners can use the log to evaluate and fine-tune their training programs. Let's see what the main benefits are.

Build a consistent record. "Keeping a training log is part of the discipline of training," says Bob Schlau, the top-ranked masters runner in the world in 1988. In other words, the habit of logging your workouts is beneficial not only as a record but also because it helps get you out the door: You don't want to end up seeing lots of blank white spaces in your log, do you?

Keep motivated. "When things seem tough, looking back through my training log can be motivational," says two-time British Olympian Jill Hunter. In fact, just writing your entries can get you psyched, like reporting in to your coach. It's easier to keep going when you see how far you've come.

Analyze what works…and what doesn't. We've all heard what happens to people who forget the past—they are destined to repeat it.

Training logs—really history books—will help you avoid making the same mistake twice. Suppose you've just had a series of poor races. What went wrong? Flipping back through your training log over the last six weeks reveals that you did two hard speed workouts a week (up from your usual one), with the second just two days before each race.

The analysis: You overtrained during the week and had dead legs during races. The solution? Cut back to one speed workout a week and add light fartlek three days before races.

But sometimes we *want* to repeat the past—like when you just knocked 25 seconds off your 10-K personal record. You might ask, what did I do right? A quick review reveals that over the last two months you've added an easy long run with a group of friends on Wednesdays. (Actually, you only started going so you could eat pizza afterward and socialize.)

Your analysis: That innocent, fun run must have brought in added aerobic conditioning you were missing in the past. Your conclusion? Keep up the Wednesday night pizza runs!

"I've kept a training log for eight years," says 1985 Boston Marathon champ Lisa Weidenbach. "I like it because I can go back and compare and figure out what went wrong or what worked."

Raise your confidence. Training logs are also an excellent confidence booster going into key races or seasons. Before Bob Kennedy, a 1992 U.S. Olympian at 5000 meters, steps on the track to race, he reviews his training log. "It reminds me of how consistent I've been in training over the past six months and that I'm now ready to race," he says.

In other words, if you've done the work in training, you'll race well. And if you've done the work and kept a log, you'll know you'll race well.

Plan for success. Instead of looking backward, use your training log to look forward. "I use training logs to plan ahead," says Budd Coates, a three-time U.S. Olympic Marathon Trials qualifier (1984, 1988 and 1992).

TIPS FROM THE TOP

TRAINING LOGS

All elite runners have plans, and a training log is the perfect place to outline those plans. Let's look at what the elites have to say about how and why they use training logs.

Steve Brace, 1992 British Olympic marathoner: "I use training logs to refer back to when things were going good—or bad."

Laurie Gomez-Henes, member of the 1995 U.S. World Track and Field Championships team at 10,000 meters: "It allows me to look back and see what seemed to work well or not work at all in the past."

Steve Holman, 1992 U.S. Olympian at 1500 meters: "I use a training log for fitness evaluation. It's good to know what you did several weeks ago, as well as in previous years. Also, by keeping a log it's easy to see your progress."

Don Janicki, 2:11 marathoner: "It's nice to look back to see what worked and what didn't. It builds confidence."

Janis Klecker, 1992 U.S. Olympic marathoner: "With a training log you can monitor improvements, trends, injuries and so on."

Anne Marie Lauck, member of the 1995 U.S. World Track and Field Championships team at 10,000 meters: "Training logs are important; they monitor how you feel and create a skeleton of how you train—what helps and what doesn't."

Lorraine Moller, 1992 Olympic Marathon bronze medalist: "I keep a

Target key races—say a marathon this fall—by penciling them in on your log. Then go back and set up your training accordingly, perhaps counting back 16 weeks from marathon race day and devising a program from there.

Need a solid six-week session to increase your speed before a summer 5-K? Map out the key workouts—say Monday and Thursday track workouts—on your log ahead of time. Then all you have to do is show up at the track on those days and put in the work.

Setting Up a Training Log

So, what do you want to record? What you write can be as simple as the date and number of miles, but there's lots more to say, if you want. Other information that can go in your training log includes:

log when I'm very focused, and read over it before my big event to reassure myself how hard I've worked."

Annette Peters, 1992 U.S. Olympian at 3000 meters: "It's nice to see all the progress. Also, if you start breaking down your training record, you can look to see the type of work you have been doing."

PattiSue Plumer, two-time Olympian (1988 at 3000 meters, 1992 at 3000 and 1500 meters): "It lets you see what works and what doesn't, to identify trends and pick up on overtraining."

Ken Popejoy, world masters champ at 1500 meters in 1991 and 1993: "As a collegiate runner, my training log was a great resource for constant reference, for fine-tuning what worked for me and making adjustments. As a masters runner, it's a more personal recollection resource."

Reuben Reina, 1992 U.S. Olympian at 5000 meters: "Once you realize what you've been doing, a training log keeps you motivated and works as a reference for future training."

Steve Spence, 1991 World Marathon Championships bronze medalist and a 1992 Olympic marathoner: "Training logs give a sense of progression. They're also good for looking back for comparison."

Jim Spivey, two-time U.S. Olympian at 1500 meters (1984 and 1992): "My log keeps my weekly mileage under control, and acts as a reference if I'm injured or if I had a good season."

- Time it took you to run your workout: 39:15
- Place: Kendall Park
- Course: trail loop
- Grade your effort: A
- Comment on effort: pushed it, felt strong
- Weather: 55°, sunny skies, no wind
- Pulse rate: 160 to 175
- Weight (before workout): 148
- When you started wearing a new pair of running shoes, to help determine the life of your shoes
- Any additional activity related to your workout: weights in health club (two sets of regular routine), 15 minutes in hot tub
- For future reference, record any injuries, treatment and time off for recovery.

TYPICAL TRAINING SCHEDULE FOR ANN MARIE LAUCK

Anne Marie Lauck's training log shows her typical workouts for a nonracing week during the competitive season. "If I race," adds Lauck, a member of the 1995 U.S. World Track and field Championships team at 10,000 meters, "I'll change my track workouts to Monday and Wednesday and do easy distance on Thursday and Friday before the Saturday race."

Sunday		12–14 mi., 6:00–6:50 pace
Monday	A.M.	8 mi., training pace (6:10–6:40)
	P.M.	5 mi., training pace
Tuesday	A.M.	5–7 mi., training pace
	P.M.	Track workout:
		3 × 1 mi. (4:50–4:55 pace) with 400 m. jog to recover
Wednesday	A.M.	5 mi., training pace
	P.M.	5 mi., training pace
Thursday	A.M.	5–7 mi., training pace
	P.M.	Track workout:
		3 sets of 4 × 400 m. (65–68 sec.) with 200 m. jog between each and 400 m. jog between sets
		4 × 200 m. with 120 m. jog recovery (29–30 sec.)
Friday	A.M.	8 mi., training pace
	P.M.	May or may not run 5–7 mi. (felt tired, so didn't run)
Saturday	A.M.	10 mi. with fartlek of 5 min. hard, 2 min. recovery
	P.M.	5 mi., training pace

The Medium for the Message

Everything from pieces of scrap paper stapled together to a preprogrammed computer disk can and does serve as a log. So do notebooks, daily planners and wall calendars—not to mention actual training log books.

Choosing a medium for your training log, like picking a running schedule, depends on your individual needs. If all you plan on is simply logging the number of miles each day, then a wall calendar (with its limited writing space) would suffice. If you want to include more information, pick something with more space, like a notebook.

And another thing: If you've tried to keep a log before and failed—because you're lazy about it—desk or wall calendars seem to work best. Why? Because they're right in front of you all the time. You don't have to log on, pick them up or even open them to record your workout. All you need is a pen or pencil and a few seconds.

Running Injuries

STAYING IN THE GAME

Just weeks before the 1992 U.S. Olympic Men's Marathon Trials, Bob Kempainen was in hot—well, lukewarm—water. Kempainen, who was recovering from stress fractures, was doing all his workouts with a wet vest in a pool. He didn't know if his two and three hour runs in the water would bring him to the fitness level needed to make the Olympic Team, but he wasn't about to hit the roads and risk reinjuring his leg—and possibly lose the next few months of training.

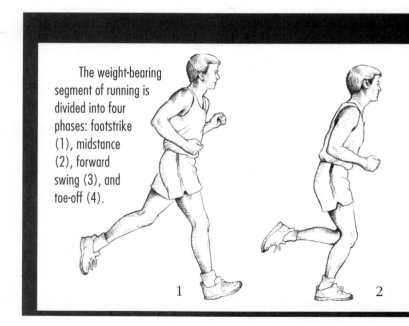

The weight-bearing segment of running is divided into four phases: footstrike (1), midstance (2), forward swing (3), and toe-off (4).

Kempainen, a med school student, is an exception among runners in that he took his time, let his injury heal and didn't try to come back too soon. The fact that he made the Olympic Team (as the third runner) was as much a tribute to his patience and self-control (attributes, by the way, of good marathoners) as it was to his undeniable talent.

And patience is a key word when dealing with injuries. Almost every runner gets injured; most, in time, will be healthy again. But an injury that should take three to four weeks to heal can end up taking twice as long if we come back too soon.

So learn from the doctor (Kempainen, that is).

Hitting Your Stride

When you run, you're a five-foot-seven or six-foot-one shock absorber. Your feet collide with the ground—1500 to 2000 times every mile—at a force of several hundred pounds, depending on your weight, your speed and the running surface.

That means . . . ouch!

All this force is absorbed by the foot and transmitted through the leg to other parts of the body, like knees, hips and your aching back. When you think about it, it's a wonder we're not sitting at home

3   4

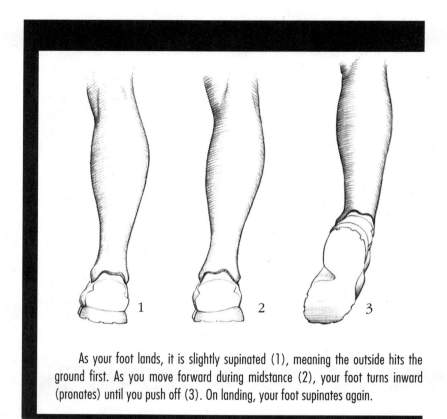

As your foot lands, it is slightly supinated (1), meaning the outside hits the ground first. As you move forward during midstance (2), your foot turns inward (pronates) until you push off (3). On landing, your foot supinates again.

every night watching *Jeopardy* with an ice pack on some part of our body. Fortunately, the body is constructed to absorb, transmit and disperse these forces during the running stride.

Injuries: What Goes Wrong

The motion of the foot in and of itself is not going to cause you to grab your knee in pain, but improper mechanics, overtraining, shoes worn as thin as rice paper, or too much running on, say, concrete or around curves will.

Genetics can also lead to running injuries (thanks Mom, thanks Dad). We may be knock-kneed, suffer flat feet or have one leg shorter than the other. These conditions can cause us to change our stride, stressing feet, ankles, knees, hips and back, and leading to injuries.

INJURIES: NO ONE IS IMMUNE

Elite runners, whose livelihoods depend on them staying healthy, employ coaches, trainers, masseuses and physical therapists to keep them injury-free. Yet, as this list shows, not even world-class runners are immune to running injuries.

ATHLETE	INJURY OR INJURIES INCURRED
Don Janicki	Achilles tendon (surgery), bone spur
Bob Kennedy	Achilles tendinitis
Janis Klecker	Stress fractures (six)
Anne Marie Lauck	Plantar fasciitis, stress fractures
Lorraine Moller	Bone spur, strains, sprains
Annette Peters	Stress fracture (femur), plantar fasciitis, compartment syndrome
PattiSue Plumer	Plantar fasciitis, stress fractures, compressed disk
Reuben Reina	Sprained ankles, Achilles tendinitis, hamstring problems
Nick Rose	Fracture of upper back, four neuroma operations, two bulging disks
Jon Sinclair	Chondromalacia patella, sciatica, Achilles tendinitis, hamstring tendinitis, plantar fasciitis
Steve Spence	Stress fractures, plantar fasciitis, shinsplints, sprains and strains, lower back and hip pain, knee pain, Achilles tendinitis, compartment syndrome

Running Injuries That Trip Up Runners

Most running injuries, if detected and treated early, can be corrected within a reasonable amount of time. An important caveat to remember for these common injuries is to always come back easy. Rushing back into a full training schedule is a sure way to usher in another injury.

TIPS FROM THE TOP

AVOIDING INJURY

Elite runners have a lot to lose from injuries and go to great lengths to stay healthy. Listen to these voices of experience.

Steve Brace, 1992 British Olympic marathoner: "I have regular soft-tissue therapy to cope with the high mileage so that recovery is aided and mentally I have the confidence."

Laurie Gomez-Henes, member of the 1995 U.S. World Track and Field Championships team at 10,000 meters: "I run moderate mileage. I run frequently on soft ground, grass or wood-chip trails."

Steve Holman, 1992 U.S. Olympian at 1500 meters: "I take preventive measures by cutting back or taking a day off, stretching, being smart and not forcing my training."

Jill Hunter, two-time British Olympian (3000 meters in 1988 and 10,000 meters in 1992): "I get a regular massage, chiropractic adjustment, wear orthotics and do stretching."

Lynn Jennings, 1992 Olympic 10,000 meters bronze medalist: "Rest, massage, no overtraining or racing. I listen to my body."

Bob Kennedy, 1992 U.S. Olympian at 5000 meters: "I change my running shoes often to avoid injury."

Janis Klecker, 1992 U.S. Olympic marathoner: "I listen to my body and cross-train. I take a day off for persistent aches and pains."

Anne Marie Lauck, member of the 1995 U.S. World Track and Field Championships team at 10,000 meters: "Know your body and the fine lines that separate normal soreness from injury. I take a sauna and hot tub every day, and I get a weekly massage and chiropractic adjustments."

Lorraine Moller, 1992 Olympic Marathon bronze medalist: "Good food, good shoes, clear reasons for what you're doing, and

Runner's knee (chondromalacia patella). It's a rare runner who hasn't had achy knees after a hard run. But it's a more serious problem when it becomes chronic. Excessive ankle roll to the inside of the foot (overpronation) causes a twisting force at the knee. When

a training program that balances hard work with sufficient recovery."

Annette Peters, 1992 U.S. Olympian at 3000 meters: "I listen to my body; when I feel body stress, I back off. When I can't get motivated to get out the door for a run, I take a day or two off; sometimes I'll swim or bike."

PattiSue Plumer, two-time Olympian (1988 at 3000 meters, 1992 at 3000 and 1500 meters): "I back off at the first sign of injury (three to five days off in a row is better than one to two months or more later). I take rest days regularly."

Reuben Reina, 1992 U.S. Olympian at 5000 meters: "I stretch regularly and cut back on training when I feel an injury coming on."

Nick Rose, two-time British Olympian at 10,000 meters (1980 and 1984) and elite masters runner: "Don't be afraid to take a day off."

Bob Schlau, top-ranked U.S. masters runner in the world in 1988: "I try to listen to my body and back off when soreness and weakness appear."

Jon Sinclair, two-time U.S. Olympic Marathon Trials qualifier (1988 and 1992): "Rest when necessary and stay away from overtraining."

Joy Smith, 2:34 marathoner: "I try to incorporate water running into my schedule. This gives my legs a break from the hard surfaces."

Steve Spence, 1991 World Marathon Championships bronze medalist and a 1992 Olympic marathoner: "Fortunately, once I overcome an injury I can recognize the signs of stress and either rest, stretch or strengthen myself before it becomes a problem."

Jim Spivey, two-time U.S. Olympian at 1500 meters (1984 and 1992): "I wear orthotics for both training and racing."

this happens, the kneecap is pulled out of alignment, stressing the ligaments surrounding it.

As a result, the runner feels pain around the kneecap during or after running and often when walking up or down stairs. Runner's knee often appears when you've upped your training load too quickly without giving your body time to adapt. In other words, you've gone too far or too fast too soon.

With proper treatment (rest, ice and wearing shoes or orthotics that limit pronation), runner's knee can be cured in about four weeks. Once the pain has subsided, a progressive resistance-exercise program should be done to strengthen the quadriceps. Straight leg lifts and leg extensions are also recommended.

Two-time U.S. Olympic Marathon Trials qualifier Jon Sinclair has felt the sting of chondromalacia patella. Sinclair headed for the weight room, strengthening his quadriceps while getting needed rest. Steve Spence, the 1991 World Marathon Championships bronze medalist and a 1992 Olympic marathoner, also works with weights to help prevent runner's knee from coming back.

One note of caution: Although cortisone injections may ease the pain of runner's knee and enable you to run again, cortisone will not correct the cause (excessive pronation), and wear and tear on the joint will continue. So avoid it.

Shinsplints (tibial stress syndrome). People in all walks of life, from women in high heels to ballet dancers to Olympic runners, have had shinsplints, a catchall term used by many doctors and runners alike to describe various conditions—most often tibial stress syndrome. Characterized by pain at the front of the leg, around the shin, shinsplints are an inflammation of the tendons or muscles.

Most often a result of overtraining (too much too soon), shinsplints may also be caused by overpronation or too much downhill running, which puts more stress on the front of the shin. Because this stress leads to a strength imbalance between the shin and the muscles in the back of the leg, pain may first be felt in the calf, later moving to the shin.

Without rest or treatment, shinsplints will persist and can progress to stress fractures of the shinbone, or tibia. Treatment depends on the severity of the injury. Cutting back on your mileage and intensity sometimes helps, along with ice, massage and rest. Treated this way, shinsplints usually disappear in four to six weeks. Stretching exercises for the calf muscles and the muscle attaching to the shin will also help eliminate the cause. If you have flat feet or weak arches—which can leave you susceptible to shinsplints—you may need better arch support or possibly orthotics.

As with any injury, just because the pain is gone does not mean you should resume a full training schedule. Come back easy, making gradual increases until you're back to your desired fitness level—and running pain-free.

Achilles tendinitis. Inflammation or damage to the Achilles tendon can cripple a runner. Yet this injury often appears mild at the start. One of the largest tendons in the body, the Achilles tendon attaches the calf muscles to the back of the heel. As you push off while running, the Achilles tendon transfers the force from the foot into the leg. Excessive stretching or pulling on the tendon causes Achilles tendinitis, an inflammation of the sheath that surrounds the tendon. If ignored, Achilles tendinitis can weaken the tendon to the point of tearing.

Pain (localized in the area just above the back of your shoe) appears gradually and may actually disappear during running, only to reappear afterward or the next morning. If not attended to early, it worsens and becomes chronic. Trying to train through a case of Achilles tendinitis is like trying to run with a broken leg: You can only do further damage.

Overpronation and oversupination can lead to Achilles tendinitis, since they place added pull on the tendon. Tight calf muscles also increase stress on the tendon; even tight hamstrings can add to the problem because of the changes they can cause in running form.

Jumping into speedwork without the proper buildup is the most common cause of Achilles tendinitis. Shoes that have a stiff upper heel cup that rubs against the tendon—or wearing racing flats or spikes, which have a lower heel cup—can also cause Achilles tendinitis.

Treatment includes rest, ice (10 to 15 minutes several times a day until inflammation is gone) and possibly some kind of anti-inflammatory medication (aspirin or ibuprofen). After the pain is gone (two to six weeks, depending on severity), regularly stretching the calf and hamstring muscles will help prevent its return.

Plantar fasciitis. Across the bottom of your foot is the plantar fascia, a network of tendons that start at your toes and attach to the heel. Inflammation here is the most common cause for heel pain in runners. During the push-off phase of running, the plantar fascia helps maintain stability, counteracting the natural supination that occurs.

Plantar fasciitis is caused by overpronation, overtraining or too much speedwork. In severe cases, it can lead to the formation of a bone spur where the tendon attaches to the heel.

Rest, ice (15 to 20 minutes daily), massage, taping, anti-inflammatory medication and wearing a heel cup may help relieve the pain, but it will return unless you correct the underlying problem. Changing shoes or wearing orthotics or a heel wedge can help overpronation. Stretching the area regularly, as for Achilles tendinitis, is also recommended.

Until completely cured, avoid hill running, hard surfaces and speedwork. If a bone spur develops, surgery may be needed, but it is not always successful and the spurs may come back. Consider surgery only after everything else has been tried.

Iliotibial band friction syndrome. Along the outside of the leg, a large tendon, the iliotibial band, extends from the hip, past the side of the knee, and attaches to the outside of the tibia, a major bone in the lower leg.

Inflammation of this tendon, iliotibial band friction syndrome, is signaled by pain and sometimes swelling over the outside of the knee. The pain, caused by the tendon rubbing over the outside of the knee, usually comes on during running and subsides quickly after running. Downhill running can aggravate the condition because of increased stress on the tendon.

This injury is usually caused by sudden increases in mileage and racing, by running on hard surfaces or with hard-soled shoes, or by too much downhill running, which can exaggerate overpronation.

Most cases can be cured in three to six weeks with ice and anti-inflammatory medication. As a last resort, injection of hydrocortisone or surgery may be recommended. Lateral stretching of the outer portion of the thigh is recommended during recovery (see hip and buttocks stretch on page 74). Orthotic devices may help to correct overpronation.

Sciatica. If you've ever felt sciatic pain, you've no doubt found it a galvanizing experience. The sciatic nerve is a large nerve that extends from the spine and pelvic area down the back of the leg. This nerve can become inflamed or pinched if the curvature of the back is increased (as a result of weak abdominal muscles or bad posture, for example), causing the pelvis to tilt slightly backward. Also, a herniated or degenerated disk may cause pressure on the nerve, resulting in sciatica.

The shooting pain is usually intense, but may be relieved by changing position to ease pressure on the nerve. Other symptoms include localized backache, soreness, or a mild tingling sensation running down the back of the leg and knee or up through the buttocks.

Treatment includes rest, massage of the buttocks and hamstrings, and heat. Stretching is recommended for improving low back and hamstring flexibility (see hamstring stretches on page 72 and lower back and hip stretch on page 73). Strengthening abdominal muscles by doing crunches also helps in correcting the problem.

Stress fractures. One of the most common overuse injuries in runners, stress fractures are caused by too much mileage, sudden increases in mileage, or running on hard surfaces such as concrete sidewalks. These small hairline fractures in the feet, leg bones and even hips are seen more often in women because their bones aren't as thick as men's. But anyone (male or female) can suffer stress fractures if they have flat feet, knock-knees or Morton's toe, where the second toe is longer than the big toe.

Pain is not usually severe, but swelling and tenderness are felt around the bone. Nevertheless, stress fractures require a complete rest from running: You have a broken bone! Doctors usually put the injured leg in a splint or cast to protect the fracture during healing. If stress fractures are caught early, healing can take from four to six weeks.

Sprains. Accidents happen. A slip on the ice, tripping over a curb or stepping on a stone can cause sprains. A sprain forces a joint beyond its normal limits, stretching or tearing the ligaments that support it. Ankle sprains are most common, especially if you run on irregular running surfaces like park trails. When you've sprained an ankle, you'll know it: It hurts! In no time your ankle will swell like a purple grapefruit.

To treat a sprain, use the RICE formula: Rest, Ice, Compression and Elevation.

- The amount of *rest* depends on the severity of the injury and ranges from a few days (for a minor sprain) to several weeks (if tearing has occurred).
- *Ice* helps control the swelling and eases the pain. Apply ice several times a day for 15 to 20 minutes at a time for the first 48 hours.
- A *compression* bandage over the sprain helps reduce swelling, and wrapping the ankle will give it added support (but don't make the wrap too tight).
- *Elevation* helps to drain off the excess fluid and reduce swelling.

Weak ankles can lead to ankle sprains, so after the pain and swelling have subsided, a strengthening program should be started to help reduce the chances of reinjury.

OVERTRAINING: WHEN MORE IS TOO MUCH

Seoul, Korea, 1988: Jacqueline Gareau's last good shot at an Olympic medal in the marathon. A former Boston Marathon winner, Gareau was in top shape and champing at the bit. Yet she didn't even make it to the starting line that day because of a bad cold—a cold that was the direct result of doing too much without adequate rest. Gareau had overtrained.

Warning signs: Stop, look and listen. Signs of overtraining can be subtle, but experienced runners who have learned to listen to their bodies are aware of the typical warnings.

- Persistent soreness and stiffness in muscles, tendons and joints
- Drops in performance (say you're running 45 minutes for 10-Ks this month as opposed to 43 minutes the past few months)
- Frequent colds, sore lymph nodes and irritability
- Constant fatigue

An easy cure. Go to the movies. Read a novel. Bake cookies.

In other words, take a day off now and then to give your body a chance to recover. Marathoner Steve Spence, for example, takes a day off every two weeks, regardless of his training. You can't lose your conditioning in one day, and you might ensure yourself more enjoyment and better performance in the future.

Grading Your Injuries

Airspeed test pilots in the Chuck Yeager mold used the term *pushing the envelope* to explain how they went faster without going too fast and risking a crash. Most running injuries occur when you have gone too fast or too far too quickly; that is, you've broken through the envelope and metaphorically crashed. When excess soreness, fatigue or strain happens, it may be a signal that your fast training pace, your high weekly mileage or the racing you've done every weekend for the past three months has finally caught up with you. Just like the test pilots, you will crash and burn.

Injuries progress through four different grades, according to Tim Noakes, M.D., author of *The Lore of Running*.

Grade one injuries result in pain a few hours after exercise (a

TYPICAL TRAINING SCHEDULE FOR NICK ROSE

Two-time British Olympian at 10,000 meters and elite masters runner Nick Rose races fast and trains smart. "I'm never afraid to take a day off," Rose says. "And I do much of my speed training on grass to lessen the pounding on my legs." Here's a look at a typical training week for Rose.

Sunday	A.M.	10 mi., steady (6:30 pace)
Monday	A.M.	5 mi., steady
	P.M.	5 mi., steady
Tuesday	A.M.	10 mi., steady
Wednesday	A.M.	5 mi., steady
	P.M.	12 × 400 m. on grass
Thursday	A.M.	5 mi., steady
	P.M.	5 mi., steady
Friday		Day off if tired
	A.M.	5 mi., steady
	P.M.	5 mi., steady
Saturday	A.M.	6 × 800 m. on grass

tightness in your right calf in the evening after each run). At this level, the problem is minor and may not even be noticed. These injuries usually don't require changes in your program, but may be the first sign of overuse and may progress to more serious problems.

Grade two injuries cause some discomfort during running but do not hinder performance (in this case, the tightness that used to crop up later is now felt during your run). Heed these early warnings—to avoid more serious injuries, look closely for the cause at this time.

Grade three injuries are more severe. The pain or discomfort limits your training and racing performance (by now your calf muscle hurts so much that it is too painful to run downhill). At this point, adjustments must be made in your training schedule, and medical advice may be needed.

Grade four injuries are so severe that running is impossible and treatment is mandatory (you can't even walk without pain).

Mistakes and Good Advice: I Told You So

Most of us, through personal experience, have watched an injury progress through all four levels until we were one of the walking wounded. Too often we tried to train through the injury, a phrase that comes back to haunt runners like the Ghost of Christmas Past. Training through more often than not causes the injury to become both chronic *and* more serious, requiring more time to heal.

There are other common mistakes we—and elite runners—can correct.

Get help sooner. Seeking medical advice early can save time and pain, but runners delay because they fear being told to stop running—as if *not running* is more painful than, say, your inflamed Achilles tendon.

Ask the right person. Talk to a medical professional instead of asking other runners for advice, because many times runners' advice is peppered with the fateful suggestion to train through it.

The best advice? Find a doctor who is also a runner, or at least knows the compulsive nature of runners, and who will do everything possible to keep you active during the healing phase of your injury (say, with water running). A medical professional will treat the cause, not just the symptoms. Treating only the symptoms usually results in the return of the injury when you start running again.

CHAPTER

8

Running Shoes

TAKE A CUE FROM THE FEET OF THE ELITE

At the 1993 New York City Marathon Arturo Barrios (running his first marathon in years, and only the second marathon in his life) started slowly, content to let others push the pace. A former world-record holder at 10,000 meters, Barrios's strategy was to hang back and then attack later in the race, utilizing his speed over the final miles.

Indeed, Barrios did finish well, passing several runners in the last miles to take third. But his goal of winning the marathon fell short—not because he ran out of steam or became dehydrated, but because of his feet. An inexperienced marathoner, he chose the wrong pair of shoes and, as a result, had a severe case of blisters.

Have you ever thought about the importance and complexity of your feet? In addition to supporting your entire body weight, your feet are the basis for proper running mechanics. Each foot is made up of 26 bones held together by over 100 ligaments, and about 20 separate muscles for the movement of over 30 joints. Two arches run across each foot: The metatarsal, or lateral, arch runs across the foot from left to right; the longitudinal, or medial, arch runs down the length of the foot.

As Barrios can attest, our feet deserve the best care we can give them. Wearing the wrong shoes or poorly fitting shoes can create problems much worse than blisters. Everyone's feet are different, so finding the right shoes is an important part of injury prevention.

A Shoe for All Seasons

Walk into a running store to look at shoes and, unless you know what you're looking for, you're bound to be confused. Running shoes have gone high-tech, with materials and features that confuse even

(continued on page 58)

TIPS FROM THE TOP

RUNNING SHOES

Top athletes have the wherewithal and opportunity to try lots of running shoes over the course of their careers. Here's what these heavy users have to say about their pet pairs.

Steve Brace, 1992 British Olympic marathoner: "I like a wide sole, especially in the heel, and a durable tread for off-road running. I also like an ample toe box and a well-supported heel cup. I like a variable lacing system with lacing eyelets that let me change my lace-up pattern. My racing shoes need to be light-weight and supportive, with an ample midsole, particularly in the forefoot area."

Laurie Gomez-Henes, member of the 1995 U.S. World Track and Field Championships team at 10,000 meters: "I like a lightweight shoe with good shock absorption and a curved last."

Steve Holman, 1992 Olympian at 1500 meters: "I like a well-cushioned shoe with stability. I have the privilege of not needing durability because I change my shoes frequently."

Don Janicki, 2:11 marathoner: "I like a good fit; it has to be snug. Comfort is everything. I don't like my foot to move around inside the shoe."

Lynn Jennings, 1992 Olympic 10,000 meters bronze medalist: "I like a light, flexible shoe. I don't need the added support or stability."

Anne Marie Lauck, member of the 1995 U.S. World Track and Field Championships team at 10,000 meters: "I want a comfortable shoe that is lightweight and wide enough for my orthotics to fit properly. I don't worry about the insoles because I take them out for my orthotics."

Lorraine Moller, 1992 Olympic Marathon bronze medalist: "I look for comfort. I like my shoes light and flexible for both training and racing."

Annette Peters, 1992 U.S. Olympian at 3000 meters: "I pronate, so I look for a shoe with stability. I also like to train in a heavy shoe so when I put on racing shoes and race, I feel light. I do wear orthotics."

PattiSue Plumer, two-time Olympian (1988 at 3000 meters, 1992 at 3000 and 1500 meters): "I like as little shoe as possible, but one that still gives me protection for both training and racing."

Ken Popejoy, world masters champ at 1500 meters in 1991 and 1993: "I look for comfort and durability. My foot is very flexible. I need a light fit and a narrow shoe with a high arch. A higher sole is preferable."

Reuben Reina, 1992 U.S. Olympian at 5000 meters: "I like a shoe with a sturdy midsole and stability. The midsole gives me the shock absorbence I need; the heel counter must provide stability."

Ric Sayre, 1983 Los Angeles Marathon winner and elite masters runner: "I like a shoe that has cushioning, especially in the forefoot, since I push off on the toe and land on the forefoot when running hills."

Jon Sinclair, two-time U.S. Olympic Marathon Trials qualifier (1988 and 1992): "I like a comfortable, flexible shoe with no special motion control, but a solid feel that supports my foot. It has to be shock absorbent in the midsole, but not stiff."

Joy Smith, 2:34 marathoner: "I wear orthotics, but my training shoes must have stability, comfort and medium weight. I use a lighter training shoe for my tempo runs."

Steve Spence, 1991 World Marathon Championships bronze medalist and a 1992 Olympic marathoner: "I can run in just about any shoe. I usually rotate about five different pairs of training shoes, wearing the ones that fit the workout and terrain."

Lisa Weidenbach, 1985 Boston Marathon champ: "I like a soft, lightweight shoe. I had stress fractures while training in hard, inflexible shoes. However, the shoe still has to be shock-absorbing."

experienced runners (and sometimes even rocket scientists). But it's not that scary: Shoes fall into general categories; once you know them, you can match up your needs with the right shoe.

Racing or training? To begin with, running shoes are meant for either racing or training and are constructed accordingly. Racing shoes are very light, with no added materials to weigh you down during competition. But training shoes need to be heavier and cushioned to withstand day-in, day-out training under all conditions and on every surface.

Shoes for the long run. Training shoes come in three basic types.

1. Lightweight shoes are softer, with a less dense midsole. Worn by lighter, faster, more efficient runners who can get away with wearing a minimal shoe.
2. Widely in demand, cushioned models offer more protection. The average runner with no biomechanical problems finds these suitable for most training. They have a broader base than lightweight shoes and the soles range in density from soft to firm.
3. Finally, shoes for stability, or motion control, offer firm support and often a wide base that prevents the foot from wobbling sideways. These heavier shoes are built to last. They help correct excessive pronation and are wide enough to accommodate orthotics (corrective devices placed inside the shoes).

Sexual preference. Do women's and men's shoes differ? Not in the materials they're made from: Women need the same support that men do, and biomechanically men and women are more similar than they are different. Generally speaking, the main difference is in shoe width, women's shoes being narrower than men's. This usually means women get a better fit with women's shoes, although sometimes men with narrow feet and women with wide feet may choose to cross over to shoes designed for the opposite sex. The important thing is fit, and that depends on the individual.

Kicking the Tires: Buying a Running Shoe

Like cars, running shoes have separate components that you need to look at before buying. Will your toes have enough room? Check the toe box. Do you need stability? Look for a wide base and a firm heel counter. Is flexibility important? Bend that midsole. To judge how these babies will run under road conditions, you'll want to

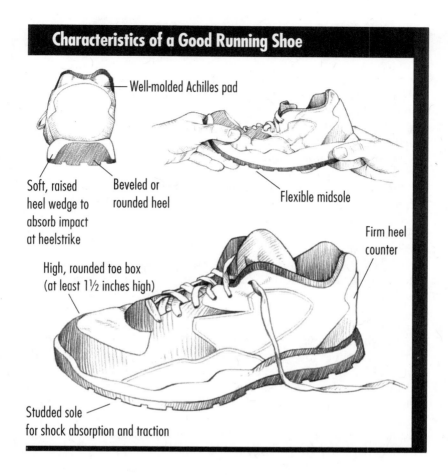

Characteristics of a Good Running Shoe

— Well-molded Achilles pad

Soft, raised
heel wedge to
absorb impact
at heelstrike

Beveled or
rounded heel

Flexible midsole

Firm heel
counter

High, rounded toe box
(at least 1½ inches high)

Studded sole
for shock absorption and traction

check out these parts and match them to your running needs.

Width: Pinch an inch. To determine proper width, try on a shoe and then pinch the upper (the outer material at the side of the shoe). If you can't get anything between your thumb and finger, the shoe is not wide enough. Very few shoes come in different widths, so try several brands to find the proper width.

Also, be sure you have an extra inch between your toes and the front of the shoe so there's room for the foot to move while running. When toes jam against the front, toenails can suffer.

Flexibility: If it ain't broken (in), don't buy it. A running shoe should not limit the foot's natural movement. A good shoe is flexible across the ball of the foot, and you can find this out even before putting it on by bending it in your hands. If it doesn't bend, don't buy it. Running shoes shouldn't have to be broken in; flexibility should be there from the start.

Shoe weight: Does it matter? If you find the right shoe with all the characteristics you need, except that it feels a little heavy, buy it. Don't sacrifice your needs for a lighter shoe; a couple of ounces will not make a difference in a good training shoe, and the extra weight actually means that the shoe is constructed more solidly and should last longer. The same applies to racing flats, but these shoes are so light that weight differences are nominal.

Outer soles: where the runner meets the road. The outer sole of a running shoe is what comes in contact with the road, and hence is where you can see the first signs of wear. If you are a heavy heel striker (the heels of your shoes constantly look like someone has taken a hammer to them), you probably need a more durable outer sole.

Normally, the outer sole should wear primarily on the extreme outer edge of the heel and in the center of the ball of the foot. An extreme pronator (whose ankles turn in) will show wear on the inside of the soles from heel to toe, with supinators (whose ankles turn outward) showing wear on the outsides of the soles from heel to toe.

Midsoles: backbone of the shoe. Perhaps the most important part of your shoe, the midsole absorbs most of the shock from your footstrike. If you are a heavy heel striker or a big-framed runner, choose a shoe with a firmer midsole. If you train constantly on hard surfaces like concrete, check your midsole every week or so by pushing on it with your thumb. It should compress and not be rigid. If it's rigid and doesn't give, the midsole has lost much of its capacity for shock absorption, which can greatly increase your chances for injury.

Insoles: close to you. The insole provides arch support and comfort during running. Improperly fitting insoles can cause blisters or foot pain across the top or side of the foot. If you wear orthotics, remove the insoles.

Toe box: under the hood. Blessed with toes as thick as Polish sausages or feet as narrow as a fork? The toe box has to accommodate these various shapes, so choose a shoe that allows enough room for your toes without causing tightness or wrinkling of the toe box when the shoe is laced. Your toes need room to move forward, but excessive movement back and forth or from side to side can cause problems.

Heel counter: bringing up the rear. The stiffness of the heel counter, which cups the back of the foot, helps control excess sideways movement (pronation and supination). If you quickly break

THINGS TO LOOK (AND LOOK OUT) FOR WHEN CHOOSING A SHOE

These guidelines are useful reminders to most runners choosing their next pair of shoes. If you're a novice and don't really know yet what you need, however, go to a running-shoe store where you can get expert advice from an experienced salesperson who is probably also a runner.

At the other end of the spectrum, if you've been running for years and know what works for you, what your idiosyncrasies are, then stick with the tried and true—don't experiment unless you're dissatisfied with your current pair.

1. Only your feet can tell you if the shoe is right. Just because the shoe is expensive doesn't mean it is better for you than the others.
2. On the other hand, if you're new at this, be willing to pay a moderate amount to get good quality.
3. Don't be influenced by an aggressive salesperson or marketing gimmicks.
4. Fitting of your shoes should only be done by someone experienced in fitting shoes properly.
5. Running-shoe size may vary from your everyday shoes, so don't insist on a particular size. And one foot may be larger than the other; in that case, always buy the size of the larger foot.
6. Your feet have a tendency to spread with age, so make sure your feet are measured each time you buy shoes.
7. Don't try to keep up with the Joneses. If you find a pair of running shoes that works for you—they're comfortable and you're running injury-free in them—don't change style or make just because another new shoe is out.
8. Don't try to keep up with the Jenningses, either. Lynn Jennings may need an entirely different shoe than you do, so don't imagine that wearing her model will make you an Olympic bronze medalist.
9. Above all, consider your special needs (body weight, shape of your feet, whether you pronate or supinate, whether or not you wear orthotics and the miles you run) before buying a shoe. A shoe has to meet your needs.

down the insides or outsides of your shoes (an indication that you pronate or supinate), you may need a shoe with a firm heel counter that provides more support and rigidity in the heel.

When Shoes Break Down

Running in worn-out shoes is an invitation to injury. So if your shoes show considerable wear—if they look like the bald tires on the

ORTHOTICS: WORTH EVERY PENNY

Strictly speaking, anything that goes into your shoe is an orthotic. But in this case we are speaking of an insert that helps to change the foot placement or the biomechanics of the gait, thus relieving pain and preventing injury. Orthotics correct the position of the foot so it functions properly—eliminating, for example, overpronation—during the running stride.

Chronic injuries, such as shinsplints or sciatica, may be caused by anatomical problems. In other words, the way you're built, particularly your feet, puts greater stress on your ankles, knees, hips and lower back when you run. Orthotics can correct these problems.

Anatomical problems of the feet plague even the elites, including Anne Marie Lauck, a member of the 1995 U.S. World Track and Field Championships team at 10,000 meters. Lauck wears orthotics—fiberglass pieces that she inserts into her shoes—to correct overpronation.

To get fitted for orthotics, you need to consult a podiatrist or other sports medicine specialist who will analyze your running stride and identify the problem. A cast of your foot is made while it's in a neutral position (relaxed, non-weight-bearing). The cast mold is then used to form the orthotic from light fiberglass or other flexible materials. Shims may be added to the orthotic to change the position of the foot and its mechanics during the support phase of the running stride to avoid overpronation. The rigidity of the orthotic will depend on the problem to be corrected.

If you are prescribed orthotics, wear them for racing as well as for training. Your street shoes may need to be fitted with an orthotic device as well, especially if you do a lot of walking or standing. Orthotics are expensive, but are worth every penny if they keep you running injury-free.

TYPICAL TRAINING SCHEDULE FOR DAN HELD

Dan Held rotates three pairs of shoes during the week: an average-weight trainer, a heavy shoe with lots of cushion and a lightweight trainer. "I use each for different types of runs, and I never use the same pair of shoes two workouts in a row," says Held, who won third place at the 1995 U.S. Marathon Championships. Here's a look at how he rotates his shoes.

Sunday		Long run in average trainer
Monday	A.M.	Easy run in heavier trainer "I like to use heavy, cushioned shoes on my morning runs when I'm not as light on my feet," says Held. "It helps absorb the extra shock."
	P.M.	Track workout in light trainer "I use less cushioning when I run fast," says Held.
Tuesday	A.M.	Easy run in heavier trainer
	P.M.	Easy run in average trainer
Wednesday	A.M.	Easy run in heavier trainer
	P.M.	Easy run in lightweight trainer
Thursday	A.M.	Easy run in heavier trainer
	P.M.	Track workout in lightweight trainer
Friday	A.M.	Easy run in heavier trainer
	P.M.	Easy run in average trainer
Saturday	A.M.	Easy run in heavier trainer
	P.M.	Easy run in lightweight trainer

used car you had in college—it's time for a replacement. What's the point of choosing a shoe with just the right features if you're going to run in it after they've worn away? Besides, by the time your shoes look worn, it's almost too late. Where the shoes break down first, and where it's most important to you, is the midsole, which is on the inside of the sole—where you can't see it. So keep track of the life of your running shoes—most midsoles break down after only 300 miles (that's ten weeks if you're averaging 30 miles a week).

If you have some extra cash, you might try this trick from the elites—rotating different pairs. For instance, Steve Spence, a 1992 Olympic marathoner, has five pairs of shoes that he wears for different workouts, depending on the terrain. He'll wear one pair for his Sunday long run on a trail, another pair for Monday's track workout, still another pair for Tuesday's easy run on a golf course, and so on.

Most of us can't afford five pairs of running shoes, but two pairs will do the trick. And an extra day of rest for your shoes will help the midsole bounce back and live longer.

To prolong the life of your shoes, heed these hints for shoe care.

- Don't wash your shoes in a washing machine. This causes them to lose their shape.
- To dry wet shoes, remove the insoles, stuff the shoes with newspaper (which holds their shape and absorbs moisture) and let them air-dry. Avoid the clothes dryer: The high heat can warp and damage the midsoles.
- Never wear your running shoes to play other sports, such as tennis, racquetball or basketball, or for aerobics class. The lateral movement of these activities can alter the balance of the shoe.

CHAPTER

9

Stretching

INDISPENSABLE FOR PEAK FLEXIBILITY

Once a week Bob Schlau, the top-ranked masters runner in the world in 1988, puts himself through an intense stretching session. He spends up to a half-hour working the various muscles (hamstrings, calves, quadriceps) of the legs until he is, in his words, "totally loose." Schlau does this in addition to daily stretching, which takes about five minutes or so, following his runs. Stretching, Schlau maintains, helps keep his stride loose and fluid, a battle that masters runners, in particular, have to fight every day.

Yet Schlau is an anomaly.

The truth is, stretching is not very popular among distance runners, elite or otherwise. Some don't stretch at all; many who stretch do so only under orders from a coach or trainer. But the truth of the matter is, stretching is the key to flexibility, which is important to every runner. Without it, your risk of muscle, ligament, tendon and joint injuries increases dramatically.

Flexibility, the range of motion around a joint, is governed by the surrounding bones, ligaments, tendons and muscles. Even though a person may be active, if a joint does not reach its full range of motion, flexibility can be reduced. In fact, a distance runner can actually become less flexible through training. Cranking out long, slow miles uses only a small portion of the total range of motion in the knees, ankles, back, hips, arms and shoulders. Muscles in these areas become tight, placing more strain on the tendons that attach muscles to bone. Eventually, ligaments, which hold the joints together by joining bones, shorten. As a result, the long distance runner often ends up with a tight lower back, hip flexors, hamstrings and calves.

And this is why two-time British Olympian at 10,000 meters and elite masters runner Nick Rose is not kidding when he says, "If I didn't stretch, I couldn't run. In fact, in the mornings I have to stretch just to walk properly."

TIPS FROM THE TOP

STRETCHING

Many elite runners admit that they don't stretch enough, but they do try. Let's take a look.

Steve Brace, 1992 British Olympic marathoner: "Stretching is especially important before morning runs. I stretch five to ten minutes daily. I use household furniture to stretch on and against, as well as steps and posts to balance against. A towel is also useful to stretch hamstrings."

Steve Holman, 1992 U.S. Olympian at 1500 meters: "I now stretch daily for five to ten minutes. I was injured last year because of inflexibility. I've been doing assisted stretching lately."

Don Janicki, 2:11 marathoner: "I stretch daily both before and after my runs. I stretch for ten minutes, but I don't do it enough. I do quad, hamstring, Achilles, calf and lower back stretches."

Lynn Jennings, 1992 Olympic 10,000 meters bronze medalist: "I stretch daily for ten minutes after running. I've never been injured. I stretch my hamstrings, Achilles, quads, calves and back."

Janis Klecker, 1992 U.S. Olympic marathoner: "I stretch daily for about ten minutes. It doesn't have to be a long session, but I do stretch after every run. I stretch arms, back, hips, hamstrings, quads, calves and feet, and also do some abdominal work."

Anne Marie Lauck, member of the 1995 U.S. World Track and Field Championships team at 10,000 meters: "Stretching is important, but

To appreciate the need for proper stretching, it helps to understand how muscle structure and function relate to range of motion. As muscles increase in strength and size, they can restrict some of the movement around the joint. This limited movement places more tension on the tendons and muscles when they are put through a greater range of motion, such as during sprinting. A typical example is the tightness often felt in the hamstring muscles and tendons behind the knees when you try to bend over and touch your toes. The hamstrings become stronger and larger through running, which may limit their range of motion. The resultant tightness in this area restricts the

I'm very erratic with it; sometimes I'll stretch daily for weeks and other times I won't stretch at all. When I do stretch, I do toe touches and stretch all the major muscles in the legs."

Reuben Reina, 1992 U.S. Olympian at 5000 meters: "I stretch daily for 10 to 15 minutes. I feel it is very important for preventing injury. I stretch major muscle groups of the legs on most days."

Nick Rose, two-time British Olympian at 10,000 meters (1980 and 1984) and elite masters runner: "I stretch daily both before and after my training for about 15 minutes."

Jon Sinclair, two-time U.S. Olympic Marathon Trials qualifier (1988 and 1992): "I stretch daily for 30 minutes. I feel it is fairly important to my training. I stretch my hams, quads, and particularly my hips and glutes."

Steve Spence, 1991 World Marathon Championships bronze medalist and a 1992 Olympic marathoner: "I feel stretching is very important both to prevent injury and for maximal performance. A loose muscle can do more work than a tight one. I use a combination of stretching and massage to loosen tight muscles. I stretch 20 minutes before a run and 10 minutes after. I also stretch according to need, depending on soreness, tightness and what I'm doing as a workout."

Lisa Weidenbach, 1985 Boston Marathon champ: "I do not stretch daily because I feel it is questionable to my training. When I do stretch, it's for hamstrings and calf muscles."

full extension of the knee that is necessary for greater speed. Consequently (after speed training, for example), runners with a limited range of motion often suffer increased muscle soreness and are more prone to muscle pulls.

How *Not* to Stretch

Remember toe touches? You did them in grade-school physical education classes. First thing after attendance you were bending over at the waist trying to touch your toes. As soon as you strained as far

MAKING ENDS MEET

Keep these guidelines in mind as you go through your daily stretching routine.

1. Choose eight to ten stretches that include both upper and lower body.
2. Always warm up first—at least five to ten minutes of light jogging—to get the most from your stretching.
3. Hold the stretch to the point of tension without feeling pain.
4. Be aware of your alignment and be sure to use proper stretching positions.
5. If possible, stretch again after your workout.
6. Stretch at least once every day.
7. Make stretching part of every workout.

as you possibly could—the kid next to you could always get farther—you bounced back up and tried again. Ten times fast. Then you went and played 30 minutes of dodge ball.

Those grade-school toe touches were usually done haphazardly and violated just about every rule of proper stretching. For starters, to maximize the benefits, stretching should be done following a proper warm-up—after some light aerobic exercise and before the major workout. If not before, then stretch after the workout: Muscles are truly warmed up then, and the benefits may be even greater.

Stretching can even be done at odd moments of the day, but take it easy. You're most likely stretching a cold muscle then, which has a shorter range of motion and therefore is more susceptible to injury.

Back to the grade-school P.E. class. You're bent double at the waist, hands about down to your ankles, head turned to the side watching the kid next to you with both hands flat on the floor. How does he do it? Your face goes red as you strain for the extra inch.

Stop! About the only thing that saved your back and legs from serious injury was the fact that you were only 12 years old. Key words for stretching are *smooth* and *controlled*. If you stretch to the point of strain, you could be doing more harm than good.

Back to P.E. class. Your hands hit the top of your canvas sneakers. That's number seven. You bounce back up instantaneously, hands flying over your head, and without another deep breath you're quickly bending over again for number eight. If you can't touch your toes like the kid next to you, at least you'll finish ten before he does.

Stop! You get almost no stretching benefit from a quick pull like that, and the constant jarring is more apt to cause a strain instead of a stretch. So another key to stretching is *do not bounce*. A static stretch ideally should be held for at least 15 seconds, and can be held up to a minute. And by the way, those toe touches you were doing are not recommended anymore because they put a lot of strain on the lower back. What used to be the standard now spells trouble.

Easy-Does-It Is the Way to Stretch

Proper stretching can help guard against soreness, muscle strains and tendinitis (inflammation of tendons). But the key point here is to make sure it's *proper* stretching. There's more to stretching than extending your legs out once or twice, reaching upward and taking a deep breath before heading out to run.

Even among those runners who do take time to stretch, many still think they need to push the stretch to the point of pain and hold it there. The philosophy of no pain, no gain does not apply to stretching, and overreaching the normal range can actually cause muscles to work against themselves and inhibit flexibility.

The reason for this is the stretch reflex. Located within the muscles and tendons are receptors that respond to stretch tension. These receptors detect muscle length and are sensitive to stretch and rate of stretch. When activated by rapid or forced stretching, the receptors

STRETCHING DEVICES: HELP OR HINDRANCE?

Have you ever noticed those ads for devices that use a rocking or tilting motion to help you stretch? Going by all sorts of names, they are usually designed to stretch the feet, ankles, Achilles tendons and calves by using body weight to place a greater stretch in these areas.

While such aids can make it easier to stretch, they also make it possible to stretch too far—to the point of pain and possible damage to muscles, ligaments and tendons.

So if you use these devices, be careful. Stretching is supposed to improve your flexibility, not cause injury. Sometimes with these devices you don't realize the degree to which you are stretching. Follow directions closely and avoid devices that do not provide proper instruction.

cause the muscle to contract or shorten (the stretch reflex), which works against the stretch.

When stretching is smooth and controlled, you should feel a comfortable tension on the muscle. Then the stretch is enhanced as the stretch reflex kicks in. Within 10 to 20 seconds, the stretch reflex subsides, allowing further extension of the muscle. This is why holding a stretch longer than the first 15 seconds is more productive than a shorter tug on the muscle.

TYPICAL TRAINING SCHEDULE FOR BOB SCHLAU

Bob Schlau, the top-ranked masters runner in the world in 1988, is almost as fast at 48 as he was at 28. One of the reasons is his stretching program. Here's how Schlau integrates stretching into his weekly workouts.

Sunday		12–18 mi., easy pace, with pickups and 5 min. of stretching
Monday		8 mi., 6:50 pace
		Stretch 5 min.
		45 sec. stretch for calves, hamstrings, quadriceps and back
Tuesday	A.M.	2 mi. warm-up and cooldown
		5 × 1 mi. (4:55 pace)
	P.M.	4 mi., easy, and 5 min. of stretching
Wednesday		9 mi. (6:50 pace) and 30 min. of stretching
Thursday		8 mi. (6:50 pace) and 5 min. of stretching
Friday		8 mi. (6:50 pace) and 5 min. of stretching
Saturday		3 mi. warm-up
		3 mi. time trial (15:10–15:20)
		3 mi. cooldown and 5 min. of stretching

Schlau's 30-minute stretching routine consists of two or three sets of these stretches: calf stretch (wall stretch), hamstring (standing and sitting), groin (sitting and modified hurdler's stretch) and quadriceps (standing).

In between each set Schlau massages tight muscles. "This session really helps my range of motion, which helps my speed," says Schlau. "It's become such a habit, I just get down and do it. I don't even have to think about it."

Stretching Routines for Runners

Flexibility increases over time as muscles are stretched regularly, but by the same token, if you stop stretching, flexibility fades very quickly. Consistency is the key. Make stretching a priority, and use it as the relaxing part of your workout. These ten stretches cover all the major muscle groups and are recommended for runners.

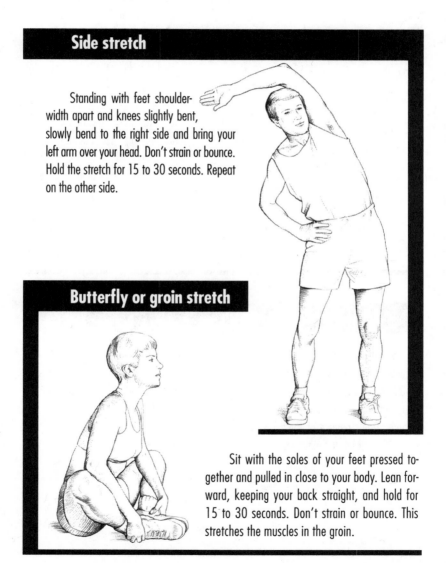

Side stretch

Standing with feet shoulder-width apart and knees slightly bent, slowly bend to the right side and bring your left arm over your head. Don't strain or bounce. Hold the stretch for 15 to 30 seconds. Repeat on the other side.

Butterfly or groin stretch

Sit with the soles of your feet pressed together and pulled in close to your body. Lean forward, keeping your back straight, and hold for 15 to 30 seconds. Don't strain or bounce. This stretches the muscles in the groin.

Achilles and calf stretch

Stand three to four feet from a wall, facing the wall, with your feet flat on the ground and parallel to each other. Place your palms on the wall and lean into it, keeping your back straight. Put one foot in front of the other, keeping your back foot pointing straight ahead and your heel on the ground. Lean forward, bending the front knee and placing your forearms against the wall. Hold for at least 15 to 30 seconds. Don't strain or bounce.

Repeat the stretch with the other leg. This stretches the calves and Achilles tendons and helps prevent shinsplints.

Seated hamstring stretch

Sit on the floor with your right leg extended in front of you. Bend your left knee and bring the sole of that foot to the inside of your right knee. Bend forward from your lower back, reaching toward your right foot until you feel a good stretch in your right hamstring. Hold for 15 to 30 seconds. Don't bounce or force the stretch. Repeat with your left leg extended.

Standing hamstring stretch

Keeping your left leg straight, place your right leg on a workout bench or chair in front of you (most runners will find that the best height is slightly below hip level). Straighten your right leg, but don't strain. To stretch the hamstring further, reach across toward your right foot with your left hand, keeping your lower back flat. Don't bounce. Hold for 15 to 30 seconds. Repeat with your left leg. This stretch eases tight hamstrings.

Lower back and hip stretch

Lie on the floor on your back with your knees bent. Slowly pull one knee toward your chin. Hold the stretch for 15 to 30 seconds. Keep the opposite foot on the floor.

Half-squat

Stand with your feet parallel to each other and about six to ten inches apart. Keeping your heels flat on the floor and your back straight, bend your knees approximately 90 degrees, or until you feel a stretch down the front of your shins. Hold for 15 to 30 seconds. Do not bend beyond 90 degrees, because full squats increase strain on the knees. This stretch helps prevent shinsplints.

Hip and buttocks stretch

Sit on the floor with your left leg straight. Bend your right knee and cross it over your left leg, placing your right foot flat on the floor along the outside of your left knee. Place your left elbow on the outside of your right knee. Slowly twist to the right, applying force to the right knee. old for 15 to 30 seconds. Repeat on the other side. This stretch helps prevent iliotibial band problems.

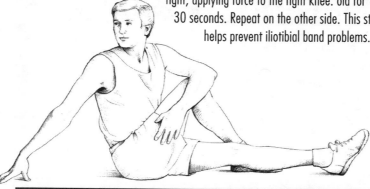

Shoulder stretch

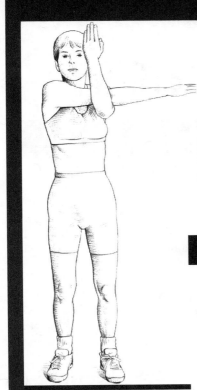

While standing, bring your right arm across your chest. Hook your left arm just above your right elbow and pull gently toward you. Hold the stretch for 15 to 30 seconds, then repeat on the other side.

Standing quadriceps stretch

Stand on your right leg and bend your left leg backward at the knee. With your right or left hand, pull up on your left ankle to stretch the front of your thigh. Bring your heel as close to your buttocks as possible without forcing the stretch. Hold for 15 to 30 seconds. Keep your back straight and your knees aligned. Repeat for your right leg.

CHAPTER

10

Mental Training

STAYING MOTIVATED

When he was a senior in college, Amby Burfoot used to rise each morning and play a song on his record player to help get him running out the door. The song was "The Impossible Dream." At the time, Burfoot was training for his own impossible dream, winning the Boston Marathon, which he did—as a dark horse—in 1968.

Todd Williams, a 1992 U.S. Olympian at 10,000 meters, heads to the track each day, where he pushes himself through tough workouts (or tough workout weeks) by reminding himself that half a world away, in Kenya, the best distance runners on the planet are working just as hard as, if not harder than, he is.

To become an elite at anything, especially distance running, you have to want it. This wanting has nothing to do with the body's physical abilities, but is part of the psychology of running. Compared with the volumes written about training the body, relatively little has been penned concerning preparation of the mind for running. Yet some have said that the mental preparation for competition is actually more important than the physical.

The truth is, mind *and* body have to work together in concert to produce outstanding performances—like winning the Boston Marathon or finishing up front in the World Championships. Even a trace of doubt in your mind about your preparation increases the chances that those fears will come true. If you believe your competitors are better prepared, you've already lost.

Mental Preparation: What Keeps Them Running

Every runner is different psychologically as well as physically. Variables such as percentage of slow-twitch muscle fibers versus fast-twitch muscle fibers (in the physical realm) and cultural, emotional and intellectual experiences (in the psychological realm) make every runner unique. And just as we would expect runners with different physical makeups to train differently—world-class U.S. steeplechaser Mark Croghan works on strength more than speed, while teammate and rival Mark Davis focuses on speed more than strength—runners with different psychological makeups get motivated in different ways, too.

Burfoot's carrot-on-a-stick was winning a particular race, the Boston Marathon. Meanwhile, Williams was motivated by thoughts of a particular group of rivals, the Kenyans. Yet even though their motivational techniques are vastly different, Burfoot and Williams have one thing in common: Each trains with a particular goal in mind.

Ready, Set, Goal!

In today's society, goal-setting has become a part of life—at home, at school, in the workplace and at leisure (like getting your handicap down in Sunday afternoon golf). Elite runners are no exception, using goals to motivate themselves to better performances, each with a different way of going about it. Take a look.

Steve Brace: I'm a full-time athlete, so money is the goal, the motivation to keep training and racing. It keeps up a standard of living for me and my family.

Barb Filutze: I sign up for future races—that gives me a goal to train for.

Laurie Gomez-Henes: My goal is improving my times, moving to the next level.

Steve Holman: I think about winning races to my competition's greatest embarrassment.

Jill Hunter: I think of some other runner out there doing more training than me, and that gets me out running.

Don Janicki: My motivational goal is simple. I pick a marathon to specifically shoot for, and then I train for it.

Lynn Jennings: I just want to be the best. That's my goal. I visualize winning over and over again.

Bob Kennedy: I'm just a very competitive person. Plus, running puts food on the table.

Lorraine Moller: I reaffirm my racing goals daily: I race to challenge myself, to break personal barriers, to know myself and to improve myself.

Sonia O'Sullivan: I like to work backward from a specific big race and set out what I want to achieve in the short term.

TIPS FROM THE TOP

MENTAL TRAINING

To be successful, it helps to have an attitude that complements your training. Elite runners find a way to keep going when the going gets tough.

Jane Hutchison, elite masters runner: "I stay motivated by wanting to stay healthy. I ran for health and fitness for ten years before I made any money at running, so staying healthy is still my true motivation."

Cathy O'Brien, two-time U.S. Olympic marathoner (1988 and 1992): "I stay motivated because I don't overrace. I'll race once a month, and on occasion twice a month, but when I do that, I know that I'll need to take a break afterward. I don't get to the point where I'm burned out mentally and physically, where my performances are starting to suffer, where mentally I don't want to run.

"And that type of thing happens a lot on the road-race circuit. I'll see people on a roll; for a couple of months they'll be racing at a really high level, then all of a sudden they're really down for a couple of months. Their race times are much slower. And that's hard for me to understand because when I'm not racing well, I won't have a great race, but I won't, say, run two minutes slower for a 10-K than before.

"Runners who are overraced have pushed it too far—go, go, go—and they're racing so much that their training has suffered. After a while, they don't even have their training to fall back on.

"Not me. I know my limits. From experience, I know that one race a month is best for me."

PattiSue Plumer: I have a major goal race each year (the national championships, for example), plus several smaller goal races along the way.

Nick Rose: I love to beat the youngsters.

Joy Smith: In planning the race season I set specific time and place goals for specific distances and events. That motivates me throughout the year.

Ric Sayre, 1983 Los Angeles Marathon winner and elite masters runner: "After 15 years on the road-race circuit, it can get to be a grind. But I've done a few things to help keep me motivated. One is I have people who I enjoy being around who I run with on a consistent basis. We run sometimes four times a week.

"Another thing for me is a good environment to train in. I like mountain trails, being off the roads and away from people and cars. That was the reason I moved from Ohio to Oregon in 1980—to change my training setting. It keeps my enjoyment level high.

"I also always have a race to get ready for. That's a big motivator because it helps me stay in reasonably good shape all year round. So I'll train with specific races—like the Parkersburg Half-Marathon and the Bobby Crim 10-miler—in mind. And while I race in the summer, I'm also slowly gearing up for the Twin Cities Marathon in the fall."

Steve Spence, 1991 World Marathon Championships bronze medalist and a 1992 Olympic marathoner: "One of the things I like to do to keep motivated throughout the year is to travel to different places to train and run with different people. Nowadays—with a wife, kids, a dog and a house—it's a little more difficult. But before I would train mostly at home, in Shippensburg, Pennsylvania, then in May go to Boulder where it's a whole new environment—really motivating with the mountains and all the world-class runners to train with. Then, toward the end of the summer, with all the college kids piling back into Boulder, I was ready to get back home to my old training environment. It kept my mind fresh."

Lisa Weidenbach: I always have a race scheduled. This keeps me going out the door to train.

Whether written in their training logs or stuck to the front of their refrigerator doors, goals like these are clearly defined in elite runners' minds. When 5000-meter specialist Yobes Ondieki jumped up to 10,000 meters in 1993, his goal was to become the first man to break 27 minutes for the 10,000 meters. Early in the year, Ondieki revamped his training to prepare for the extra 3.1 miles of racing. A few months later, with his goal clearly in mind, he ran an early-season road race to test his fitness, then dropped down to run 5000s on the track to hone his speed.

Finally, on a magical July 5 night in Stockholm, Ondieki put it all together. He ran behind a pace-setter for the first part of the race (the better to reach his goal). The last two miles he ran alone. Ondieki crossed the line in 26:58, a world record by nine seconds. The first man to break 27 minutes, Ondieki achieved his goal.

Avoiding Burnout

Because many elites are full-time runners, the temptation is sometimes simply too great to train hard—and race—all the time. Eventually, they reach a state known as burnout—they'd rather walk across hot coals than jump in a 5-K for fun. Burnout usually comes after a bad race or a series of bad races—not only is the body tired of running, but the mind is tired as well.

At this point the options are clear: Either take a temporary break or face the consequences. Instead of getting frustrated, use your setbacks as learning experiences. Many smart elites opt for a change of pace. They take a few days or weeks off, sleeping later, reading a good book or going to the movies. They break their training diet, splurging on an onion and peppers pizza. Or they cross-train: Swimming or biking refreshes not only the legs but the mind as well. Some go on vacation. Steve Spence, the 1991 World Marathon Championships bronze medalist and a 1992 Olympic marathoner, periodically escapes to West Virginia, where he owns a cabin, to de-train (that is, go fishing) after a hard race or series of races.

If an elite athlete keeps training and racing hard, however, a breakdown—physical or mental, or both—is inevitable. World-class masters miler Ken Sparks has firsthand experience. Back in the 1970s he was an elite half-miler, running a pro track circuit. "I'd train hard every day and then drag myself home, exhausted," Sparks recalls. "Running was everything. And it was a great feeling then because my racing was going well. But after a few years my times started to get slower because of age—I was in my early thirties—and soon my motivation flagged. The hard training and racing—which I made the focus of my life—was not as stimulating as it once was either. It was a chore. And one day I found myself not even wanting to jog around the block! So I quit running. Cold turkey. And for almost seven years I didn't run, until I was 40 years old, overweight and feeling old."

Sparks got his running back on track by balancing his training

NORTH MEMORIAL
WHIZ BANG RACE

1604

MARATHON SPORTS

new balance ®

RAINBOW RACING SYSTEM® 1982 · P.O. BOX 18310 · SPOKANE, WA · 800-962-1011 · www.RAINBOWRACING.com · MADE IN THE U.S.A.

ON YOUR MARK: STARTING-LINE PSYCHOLOGY

It's Patriot's Day in Boston. As the elite runners crowd forward toward the starting line, let's see what some of them are thinking.

Jane Hutchison: I'm telling myself, "I really want to get tough. I'm *not* just going to dog this race. Get tough!"

And when I say that to myself, I really believe I can do it.

Cathy O'Brien: I'm telling myself there's no pressure. Just go out and feel good and run hard. Just let it happen.

I tend to be the kind of person who doesn't like to put too much pressure on myself. I won't predict I'll win—even in my mind—and I definitely won't say that to anyone. But I will say I'm going to do the best that I can, and that keeps me from being overstressed. Simply put, I accept the fact that I'm going to run the best I can based on the training I've done.

Ric Sayre: I'm thinking that I just want to do as well, if not better, than I did at this race last year. But I'm also looking at the competition. When I start the race, I don't want to get so far behind the lead pack that I lose contact.

I'm also telling myself that I want to go out and hit that level without going over the edge. "That level" means staying comfortable even though I'm pushing myself and running hard, so I won't have to back off a mile down the road. I'm telling myself to be aggressive, but not too aggressive.

with his family life and career, but the lesson is clear: He lost seven good running years—not because he was injured and couldn't run, but because he didn't feel like it. He'd fallen victim to a major-league case of burnout.

To get the most out of running means setting goals and priorities in your life. Integrating your everyday activities with your running helps balance your psychological needs with the physical.

Break It Up: Fighting Monotony

Less severe than burnout but still a motivational problem among elites is the inevitable monotony of training: 6:00 A.M. alarm...out the door for 8 easy miles around the park...in the evening 8 to 12 miles on the trail...except Tuesdays and Thursdays when I go to the track...day in, day out...seven days a week, 52 weeks a year...the alarm clock's ringing!

TYPICAL TRAINING SCHEDULE FOR CATHY O'BRIEN

For Cathy O'Brien, rest is the key to staying motivated. "When I'm rested, I'm physically and mentally prepared to race," explains O'Brien, a 1988 and 1992 U.S. Olympic marathoner. "I generally race once a month, and this schedule is typical for that week. On my nonracing weeks I add an interval workout on Wednesday. And since I'm not racing, I cut down to one rest day those weeks."

Sunday		long run (16–22 mi.)
Monday	A.M.	10 mi., 6:45 pace
	P.M.	5 mi., easy (7:00 pace)
Tuesday	A.M.	10 mi., 1 to 2 min. pickups on the road
	P.M.	5 mi., easy
Wednesday		16 mi. (medium-long run), 6:30 pace
Thursday		6 mi., easy (rest day)
Friday		6 mi., easy (rest day)
Saturday		Race: 10-K

Pretty soon, if you're not careful, training can start to feel like an assembly-line job. Most elites avoid monotony by breaking up the routine in a variety of ways.

Change the scenery. Vary your running routes, getting off the road or track for a while and onto a mountain path or parkway.

Lighten up. Wear racing shoes during some of your easy runs; the lighter shoe sometimes helps heavy-leg syndrome, which can come with monotony.

Use your imagination. Often, elite runners play mind games—imagining themselves competing and winning a race—as motivation. Use these kinds of images to inspire your own running as well.

Pick a partner. Run with a training partner to pick up your pace and your interest. Steve Spence (first in the 1992 U.S. Olympic Marathon Trials) and Steve Taylor (sixth in the marathon trials) periodically get together for intense one- or two-week training sessions.

Go for a change of climate. Many elite runners change training bases if they can afford it, moving to places like Colorado or Florida and then back to home base. You may not be able to take off for months, but in a brutal winter, a week's vacation in a warm climate may give you a real boost. For others, a week in Canada during August can spark a lively change.

Hit the sack. Taking naps can help. Jon Sinclair, a 15-year veteran of the road-race circuit, is a famous napper. An afternoon nap refreshes not only the body but the mind as well.

Count your blessings. Remember the last time you were waiting out some minor (or not so minor) injury? You would have given anything to be able to lace on those shoes and hit the road. Sometimes this recall rekindles that desire to run.

Jog down memory lane. Finally, just remind yourself of your initial reason for running: the pure pleasure it provides both physically and mentally. Then head out the door to experience it.

CHAPTER

11

Cross-Training

From Cycling to Skiing

Runners first became aware of the concept of cross-training during the triathlon/biathlon boom of the 1980s. They watched Mark Allen's 2:40 marathon at the end of the IronMan Triathlon. They saw Ken Souza run 14-minute 5-Ks on the back end of run/bike/run biathlons. And many decided that maybe there was something to be gained, running-wise, from other sports.

But cross-training's roots extend farther back than a decade. Try a century. Way back in the 1850s, British distance-running ace Captain Barclay used six-mile walks as a part of his daily training. The first man to break four minutes for the mile, Roger Bannister, was fond of rock climbing during the competitive season. Sebastian Coe, who after more than 13 years is still the world-record holder in the 800 meters, used plyometrics—bounding and jumping drills—in his pre-season buildup. And masters-record holder Derek Turnbull of New Zealand has worked full-time on his sheep farm for 30 years, lifting and shearing sheep during the day and then going for long runs in the evening.

The Benefits of Diversity

Not all elite runners cross-train. Some maintain that only running will help their running. As a result, they avoid the pool (and the bike, and the stair-climber...). But among elite runners who cross-train, top choices include cycling, swimming, water running, cross-country skiing and aerobics—sports that build endurance. Using other sports can help a runner in many ways.

Building strength. No one sport will work all muscles, so by alternating between running and another activity you optimize your conditioning. Stronger quads from cycling, for example, will balance the powerful hamstrings that come from running. (Strength training

84

with weights is not considered as cross-training here, but as an accompaniment to running. For further discussion of weight training, see chapter 4.)

Increasing overall fitness. Cross-training can also supplement your running and help enhance your cardiovascular endurance.

Injury prevention and recovery. An alternative sport can give one set of muscles a break so they don't wear down as quickly. And if you do get injured, your new workouts—in the pool, for example—will keep you fit while allowing you to heal.

Variety. A change in the routine can help keep you from getting stale or bored. Something new adds freshness to your workouts so you can be ready to run.

Why Runners Cross-Train

Individually, the runners interviewed for this book gave different answers for why they cross-train. Those answers are summarized here.

1. *It's better than nothing.* Some cross-train only when injured—it's a poor second to running, they feel, but at least they maintain fitness while healing.
2. *To stay strong without wearing out.* Another group cross-trains regularly so they won't break down in the first place. The change keeps them from getting injured by avoiding too much stress on the body in the same way every day.
3. *The variety keeps them fresh.* During the off-season or for a break from running at any time, cross-training can help recharge your batteries. After a long training season you need a break, but doing nothing gets old fast. By switching to biking or in-line skating, for example, runners stay fit and give their legs a break from the constant pounding on the roads.
4. *All of the above.* And, of course, some runners cross-train during the season because they like the variety and want to balance themselves by strengthening muscles and joints not used much during running.

Let's look at some personal experiences from two top runners.

Bob Kennedy, a 1992 U.S. Olympian at 5000 meters, spent the spring of 1994 on a stationary bike rather than on the roads. A stress fracture kept him from running, and for six weeks, while it healed, Kennedy did his best Greg LeMond impersonation, bicycling about

TIPS FROM THE TOP

CROSS-TRAINING

Some elite runners don't need an injury, or the threat of one, to get them to a pool, on a bike or in an aerobics class. They make cross-training part of their training routine. These elites who cross-train present a good case for not running all the time. Here's what some regulars say about it.

Lorraine Moller, 1992 Olympic Marathon bronze medalist: "Three times a week I'll run the pool for about an hour. I do those workouts in the mornings—Mondays, Wednesdays and Fridays—in place of morning runs. My pool work is a social time for me; I go with a friend. But it is also a good workout. I equate an hour in the pool to an hour running.

"What I do is simple. I put a vest on and get in the deep end and start running. (At my pool in Boulder, they now have lanes reserved for water running.) I use the same motion I use on land, and if I want a harder workout I take the vest off and run without it. I have to build up to that, because running without the vest is hard work. The first time I'll take my vest off for 10 minutes, the next time 20 minutes, and so on.

"I like water running because I feel I'm getting resistance from the water in every part of my stride. It's a lightweight workout in that respect, and it works my upper body as well.

"Being in the water gives me some relief from the pounding my legs take on the roads, but I still feel I'm getting in the miles. And the movement tends to act like a light massage, flushing stuff out of the legs, so it's beneficial on several counts. I've been water running for five years; I think it's one of the things that helped me win the bronze medal in 1992, and it continues to help prolong my racing career today."

PattiSue Plumer, two-time Olympian (1988 at 3000 meters, 1992 at 3000 and 1500 meters): "Two mornings a week I do low-impact

two hours a day. But it did heal, and Kennedy did maintain his fitness level and aerobic conditioning over that time—so much so that come summer, Kennedy ran the second-fastest U.S. 5000 ever, a personal record by more than ten seconds.

Masters runner Ric Sayre has run too many miles to count. Today, aerobics. It's a class at the local health club that lasts for 90 minutes, and I use it to replace a morning run.

"Low-impact is the key, because no matter how slow you go when you run, after 20 minutes your muscles start breaking down. I was looking for something that would give me a workout and not break me down, and I found aerobics. (Cycling tends to overdevelop my quads, and where I live in California all the pools are outdoors; when it's 50° in the morning, I don't want to jump in the water!)

"With aerobics I don't overdevelop any particular muscle group—and I stay warm. I get a lot of side-to-side action, which is good for the abductors and the adductors (outer and inner thigh). It's a total-body workout, and I feel that the stronger you are, the better runner you will be.

"Aerobics is also fun. It's a group activity, which is different from most of my running workouts."

Ric Sayre, 1983 Los Angeles Marathon winner and elite masters runner: "In season, once or twice a week I'll go mountain biking on forest roads. I ride whatever course and distance I feel like, but usually it's about an hour or an hour-and-a-half ride up some pretty challenging hills.

"It's easier on my legs because I don't get the pounding, but the rides are still intense. I ride hard, pushing myself the whole way. I can really feel it in my quadriceps and in my lungs when I'm pedaling a 30-pound mountain bike up a forest road that climbs 1,000 feet. It's a short, but hard, workout.

"I started riding about five years ago, and I've found that one or two rides a week is a good complement to my running; if I start doing any more than that, biking tends to tighten up my legs and is detrimental to my running, so I stick with one or two rides a week."

he cycles a couple of times a week, not only for variety but also to escape the pounding of running.

Cross-training not only keeps you from pushing yourself too hard on the road by giving your body a much needed rest, it also strengthens certain body parts that are prone to injury. Knee pain, common

TYPICAL TRAINING SCHEDULE FOR RIC SAYRE

As a second workout of the day, Ric Sayre uses mountain biking. "I'll have run 10 to 14 miles in the morning, and sometimes I'm on my feet five or six hours at work, so bike riding is a good replacement for a 5- to 7-mile run in the evening," says Sayre, the 1983 Los Angeles Marathon winner and an elite masters runner.

Sunday	A.M.	18–20 mi., easy pace
Monday	A.M.	7–10 mi., easy
Tuesday	A.M.	13 mi., easy
	P.M.	90-minute mountain bike ride
Wednesday	A.M.	5–7 mi., easy
	P.M.	3 mi. warm-up; 6 × 400 m., with a 200 m. rest between; 2 mi. cooldown
Thursday	A.M.	10 mi., easy
	P.M.	60 min. mountain bike ride
Friday	A.M.	7–10 mi. easy
Saturday	A.M.	Race or tempo run (8-K to half-marathon)

in runners who up their mileage or intensity, often results from an imbalance between overdeveloped hamstrings and underdeveloped quadriceps. Cycling is a perfect cross-training exercise to ward off this problem because it develops the quadriceps like no amount of running ever could.

Recharging Your Batteries: When You Don't Feel Like Running

At some point even elite runners tire of putting one foot in front of the other. At the end of, say, the fall European track season or a four-month buildup that culminates with a marathon, many take a few weeks off, doing nothing but reading and watching TV. This is rest and recovery time, and the recliner gets more work than the Reeboks.

Lately, though, more elites are turning to cross-training during this downtime.

Why? Because they've found that cross-training gives them the physical rest and mental escape from running they need while keeping the body in relatively good shape. They're having their cake and eating it, too.

Ric Sayre rides his mountain bike three or four times a week during his time off from running. Lisa Weidenbach heads for a pool when she's feeling unmotivated. Laurie Gomez-Henes plays tennis.

And because they cross-train, when the time comes (two to eight weeks down the line) to start serious running again, they're not back to the drawing board in terms of their fitness level. "Cross-training during recovery weeks makes it easier to get back into running again," says Sayre.

CHAPTER

12

Treadmill Running

THE ADVANTAGES OF INDOOR WORKOUTS

Back in 1980, Benji Durden had a secret. The soon-to-be Olympic marathoner was sneaking over to the exercise physiology lab at Georgia Institute of Technology in Atlanta to work out on a treadmill. At the time, treadmills were used primarily for testing VO₂ max. "I didn't tell other runners I was using a treadmill," recalls Durden. "They would have thought I was a little strange. Heck, even the lab guys thought I was a little nuts."

Reasons to Tread Ahead

Today, however, almost every elite runner has logged a few miles on a treadmill—and many swear by them. Treadmill running enables you to:

Stay off thin ice. It's January in Minnesota, and the scenery outside looks like outtakes from *Ice Station Zebra*. So you head to the rec room, pop a *National Geographic* special about the Fiji Islands in the VCR, then step on your treadmill—and feel warmer immediately.

Severe winter weather, the most obvious reason to use a treadmill, brings more than blustery winds and low temperatures—it can be downright dangerous. Ice patches and bad drivers can make winter runs hazardous to your health. So why not stay inside? Many elites do.

"I don't mind the cold too much," says Minnesota's Bob Kempainen, American-record holder in the marathon. "But if it's slippery, I'll get my ten-mile run in on a treadmill. Why risk it?"

Beat the heat. Severe heat is another reason to hightail it to the health club or wherever there's a treadmill inside. Top masters runner Carol McLatchie, who lives in Houston (where you can melt your outsoles on the concrete during the summer), keeps her treadmill on an enclosed back porch next to an air conditioner. She does several workouts a week there. "The air conditioner is just a small window unit," she says. "It gets the temperature down to 80°F. And that's a lot better than the 95° in the sun!"

Dovetail a run with other obligations. Job and family restraints put pressure on elite runners, just as they do for everyone else. Sometimes a quick run on the treadmill is the only way to fit in a workout and still deal with closing time at the shoe store, Junior's dental appointment and dinner out with the spouse.

Durden, who coaches several runners by fax and phone, remembers a particularly busy month when he lived on the treadmill in his office. "I did 23 days in a row on the treadmill," he says. "I was afraid that if I went out on a long run for an hour or two, I'd miss a lot of calls. It was either that or take a cellular phone with me. And I didn't know how well the cellular phone would work when it got all hot and sweaty."

Budd Coates, a three-time U.S. Olympic Marathon Trials qualifier who also serves as fitness director for Rodale Press, recalls an evening workout done on a treadmill while watching his baby daughter. "I didn't get a chance to run during the day because of work," he says. "So I brought my daughter in and sat her down next to the treadmill. The rhythmic sound of my running on the treadmill put her to sleep." (Coates, however, cautions parents: "The belt of a treadmill is like a spoke on a wheel. It's a temptation for children to put their fingers and hands in there, so be careful.")

Stay healthy. World-class masters miler Ken Sparks recommends treadmill training to come back from injuries or to avoid them altogether. "First of all, there's less pounding of the legs on a treadmill than on the roads," says Sparks, "because the treadmill belt gives when you land on it, unlike concrete and asphalt.

"Second, there's no side slope on a treadmill as there is on roads. That slope forces you to overpronate and can lead to shinsplints, Achilles tendinitis and knee problems.

"And third, on a treadmill you avoid the lateral (sideways) pressure on your knees and ankles that occurs when you run around a track. Lateral pressure is tough on joints and can lead to injuries."

Set a precise pace. Sparks also likes treadmills because they're precise. "It's a much more evenly paced workout than running on a track," he says. "For instance, if you're doing 400-meter repeats on a track in 90 seconds, you might run the first 200 in 43 seconds and the second in 47. On a motorized treadmill—which will run at an even pace—you can't do that. Each 200 will be in 45 seconds."

Program your hills. Hill workouts on the treadmill offer a special opportunity for McLatchie and 2:34 marathoner Joy Smith, Houston denizens who otherwise would have to drive 90 minutes to find an incline made by Mother Nature.

Even Durden, a Colorado resident, prefers to run hills on a treadmill. "You can replicate your hill sessions from week to week almost perfectly," says Durden. "With some of the fancier treadmills, you can program in your workout. If you want to do a 2 percent grade and a 1 percent recovery, you just punch some buttons. It's very precise and easy to do."

Simulate racecourses. Computerized treadmills come with built-in programs that take you up and down hills, increase the pace and slow the pace during your run. They also let you program your own courses.

Colorado's Matt Carpenter trained on a treadmill for the Mount Washington Road Race in New Hampshire. Carpenter programmed the exact grade of the ascent and set the pace slightly faster than the course record. Carpenter won the race but missed the record by 33 seconds on a day when rain made the footing slick. "You can't put mud on a treadmill," he says with a shrug.

McLatchie and Smith ran up and down hills before the 1993 Boston Marathon at precisely the grade and length of the Newton Hills, including Heartbreak Hill—on their treadmills. Ditto for the U.S. 1992 Women's Olympic Trials. Even though the trials were held in Houston, McLatchie and Smith didn't want to beat themselves up running the mostly concrete course several times before the actual race. So they programmed the last six miles of the race—where freeway ramps provide the only hills on the course—into their treadmills.

"We ran the workout on the treadmill once a week for three months before the trials," says McLatchie. "We'd run outside to fatigue our legs, then hit the treadmill for the six-mile program. During the actual race we felt that our legs knew those hills."

Beating Boredom

We've all heard the complaint "What could be more boring than running on a treadmill?" Quite a few elite runners who work out on treadmills won't argue with you on that point. Instead, they'll tell you how they've gotten around it.

Ken Martin, runner-up at the 1989 New York City Marathon, blasts the B-52s on his six-CD stereo system while on a treadmill. Durden watches videos of previous Olympics. McLatchie's treadmill

HOW TO USE A TREADMILL

Learning to run on a treadmill is like learning to ride a bike. Once you get the hang of it, it's easy. The first few times on a treadmill can be awkward, so even elite runners start off slowly to get used to the feel of running fast but not actually moving forward.

If you try one out in a store or a health club, someone will be there to walk you through the process. But the basics of treading safely are quite simple.

1. Read the instructions.
2. Straddle the sides of the belt when starting the machine; don't stand on the belt.
3. Start slow.
4. Hold the side rails as you step on and as you make any changes (such as increasing the incline or speed).
5. Bring the incline and speed back down before you stop.
6. Know where the emergency button is.

Even with regular use, many elites experience a difference in their treadmill workouts. "When I'm on the treadmill, I always have this feeling that I'm going faster than on the roads," says McLatchie. "I just don't have the visual cues—like scenery going by—and I think that throws me off a bit.

"Another sensation is that when I stop, my equilibrium is off. Something is still moving. It's like I was out at sea, and now I'm on land again. I have sea legs for a few minutes."

is next to a window that looks out on her backyard. Smith has a full-length mirror in front of her so that she can monitor her running form. And no matter what Carpenter does on his treadmill, he does *not* look at his watch! "If I look at my watch, time seems to go really slowly on a treadmill," says Carpenter.

If sounds and sights aren't distraction enough, find something more compelling. Many elite runners throw in a little pain.

"I never get bored on my treadmill," says Sparks, who treadmill-trains alongside garden hoses, rakes and shovels in his garage. "That's because I know that when I step on my treadmill, I'm going to be doing an intense speed workout." Similarly, Don Janicki's treadmill sits isolated in his basement. "I know that when I go down there it's going to be a tough workout," he says. "I actually look forward to it."

Adapting Outdoor Workouts

Elites can do practically any outdoor workout inside on a treadmill.

Long runs. Prior to his 2:09:38 second-place finish at the 1989 New York City Marathon, Ken Martin logged all his long runs on a treadmill. "I'd just get into a nice rhythm and stay controlled," he says. "I also liked having my water bottles right there beside me so I didn't have to stop to drink."

Tempo runs. Durden still remembers a structured tempo workout he did on a treadmill in 1980. "It was at a lab in Missoula, Montana, where they were testing shoes for Nike," he says. "In two days I ran 14 workouts of eight minutes each at a 5:00 pace. I was extremely efficient on the treadmill. Two weeks later, I made the Olympic Team in the marathon."

Joy Smith often covers 10 to 12 miles on her treadmill, but she breaks up the monotony by throwing in two or three 2-mile tempo runs. Coates likes to set his treadmill at a 5:00 pace and cruise for 5 to 15 minutes. "It's actually kind of relaxing," he says. "You don't have to check your splits; you don't have to concentrate on keeping your pace. If you drop off your pace, you're off the back of the treadmill."

Speed. Ken Sparks has been running speed sessions on a treadmill since the late 1960s, when he was a graduate student at Ball State University in Muncie, Indiana. "I didn't have much time back then, and some of my workouts would actually be jumping on a treadmill, warming up, running a 4:00 mile and then jumping off. The workout was short and I'd go back to work," he says.

Nowadays, on his homemade treadmill, Sparks clicks off 62-second quarter-miles with a one-minute rest in between. (Most commercial treadmills don't reach this speed: See the discussion on what to look for in a treadmill later in the chapter.)

Hills. "Treadmills can really give you a workout," says Janicki, who runs hill sessions on his treadmill. A favorite starts with a 15-minute warm-up. Then he sets the incline to the desired grade (say 3 percent) and runs 3 minutes on the grade, then jogs 1 minute on the flat; next, 2 minutes up and a 1-minute jog on the flat; 1 minute up and a 1-minute jog on the flat. He repeats the series three times, running according to how he feels, with a 15-minute cooldown.

Test Driving a Treadmill: What to Look For

Treadmills offer a variety of features and come in two basic types: motorized and nonmotorized. Motorized treadmills, which tend to

TIPS FROM THE TOP

TREADMILL WORKOUTS

Several elite runners have developed specific treadmill workouts that work well in their training schedules.

Matt Carpenter, Pike's Peak Marathon champion: "Warm up for 30 minutes on the roads. Set the treadmill to 11.5 percent grade and run three miles at a 7:00 pace, then a couple of minutes easy. At flat grade, run 4 × 1 minute at a pace equivalent to pace for 400-meter repeats (60 to 65 seconds), with 1-minute rest intervals, running at 6:00 pace in between. Cool down for 30 minutes outside."

Benji Durden, coach and 1980 Olympic marathoner: "Warm up for four miles (8:00 to 6:40 pace). Then, holding 6:00 pace, run 0.7 mile at 2 percent uphill grade and 0.3 mile at 1 percent downhill grade, then repeat this pattern until you've covered 6 to 8 miles. Cool down for 3 to 4 miles."

Carol McLatchie, masters runner: "Warm up for two miles (8:00 to 7:00 pace). Off the treadmill do some light stretches, then four strides at 5:30 pace (pickups of 100 to 150 meters for 15 to 20 seconds each) to open up legs. Jog a minute; run a 5:30 mile; three minutes at 7:00 pace; 1200 meters at 5:20 pace; three minutes easy; 800 meters in 2:36; three-minute rest; 400 meters in 0:76. Cool down for two miles."

Joy Smith, 2:34 marathoner: "Warm up for two miles (7:00 to 8:00 pace). Run three miles (6:00 pace); one mile at 5:30; two miles at 11:30; another 5:30 mile; two miles in 12:00. Cool down for two miles."

be more expensive, turn the belt at a set speed, which the runner must match. With a nonmotorized treadmill, the runner dictates or controls the speed with his stride. The energy cost of running is higher. "I prefer the nonmotorized kind," says Don Janicki, who has been treadmill training for three years. "But you can get a good workout on either one."

Once you've made that choice, the following treadmill features should be considered. These characteristics are important to all runners, including the elites.

BELTS VERSUS THE ROADS: THE COST OF RUNNING

Despite their many advantages, do treadmills give you as good a workout as running on the roads? How does the work compare? According to some researchers, treadmill running requires about the same amount of energy as running outdoors.

The difference is the wind resistance. When running outside, any breeze blowing against you adds resistance and increases the energy cost of running. Plus, you create wind resistance as you move through any distance. On the treadmill, without wind resistance, energy cost is slightly lower.

To compensate for this difference, a runner could elevate the treadmill 1 to 2 percent. Ken Sparks, world-class masters miler, prefers to increase the speed slightly to increase energy cost and at the same time increase leg turnover.

Belt size. Not all runners, even elites, have perfect strides. A narrow belt (20 to 24 inches)—the part of the treadmill that you run on—may cause problems for runners with wide or awkward footstrikes. If you make contact off the belt—the part that's not moving—you can take a tumble, so it's best to thoroughly test-run a treadmill to be sure it accommodates your stride. After all, many times you're running on a treadmill so you won't have to worry about footing—when it's icy and snowy outside, why bring the worry indoors with you?

Top speed. Nonmotorized treadmills will go as fast as you can. Top speeds on motorized ones range from 8 miles per hour (7:30 pace) to 12 miles per hour (5:00 pace). Most elites don't do all-out speedwork on their treadmills, so the motorized ones are fine. But most of those who do fast repeats (60- to 65-second quarter-miles) use nonmotorized machines.

Stability. When you push the pace, some lightweight treadmills vibrate like a cheap compact car at 65 miles per hour. If speed is a concern on your treadmill, find one that doesn't hop across the room as you run on it. Some give is good because that means it's absorbing shock, but a heavier machine that's anchored well is preferable.

Elevation change. Hillwork is another reason many elites take to their treadmills. Most treadmills have elevation-change switches that will take them from running flat to charging up the Newton

TYPICAL TRAINING SCHEDULE FOR KEN SPARKS

Ken Sparks, world-record holder in the 800 and 1500 meters (age groups 45 to 50 and 50 to 55), uses the treadmill to pace himself precisely for speed workouts.

Sunday	A.M.	5 mi., easy pace
	P.M.	5 mi., 5:30–5:45 pace
Monday	A.M.	7.5 mi., 6:00–6:15 pace
	P.M.	4 mi. treadmill, 5:50 pace
Tuesday	A.M.	6.5 mi., 6:00–6:15 pace
Wednesday	A.M.	5 mi., easy
	P.M.	Treadmill workout:
		2 mi. warm-up, 6:00 pace
		8 × 440 m. (62 sec.); 1 min. rest between
		8 × 220 m. (31 sec.); 1 min. rest between
		1 mi. cooldown
Thursday	A.M.	7 mi., easy
Friday	A.M.	7 mi., 6:00–6:15 pace
	P.M.	4 mi., easy
Saturday	A.M.	5 mi., easy
	P.M.	Treadmill workout.
		2 mi. warm-up, 6:00 pace
		440, 880, 440; repeat sequence; 70 sec. pace
		1 min. rest between each
		1 mi. cooldown

Hills. Grades generally top out at 12 to 15 percent.

Some, like the treadmill Smith and McLatchie share, even go downhill. That's good when you want to practice that neglected part of road racing—or teach your legs a faster tempo than on the flat.

Surface. Not all treadmill belts are the same. Some are wider than others, and some offer more cushioning for easier impact, using thicker rubber for the belts, shock absorbers under the belt and aluminum frames that bend more than steel frames do on impact.

Again, one of the reasons many elites turn to treadmills is for a respite from the pounding on concrete. The running surfaces of treadmills are not as hard as the sidewalk, but they vary in shock absorption, so each runner needs to find a surface that's right for him.

Programs. Not all treadmills—even the motorized ones—have this option. But elites, like McLatchie and Smith, use this feature quite often, plugging in the uphill and downhill grades at upcoming road races and simulating those courses in their dens.

CHAPTER 13

Training and Racing in the Heat

DRINKING FLUIDS TO KEEP COOL

Late in the 1994 Revco/Cleveland Marathon, the Ukraine's Lyubov Klochko and Hungary's Karolina Szabo were locked in a two-woman duel for first place. Temperatures were in the high 60s that day, and the humidity was way up. With three miles to go, Szabo suddenly dropped off the pace. Klochko went on to win easily in 2:36:13. When Szabo crossed the line two minutes later (2:38:16), she immediately dropped to the pavement. Szabo was carried to the medical area where she stayed for an hour, getting intravenous fluids to combat dehydration.

Heat injuries are common in running, and elite runners are not exempt. It would be nice to always train and race when the temperature was a comfortable 50° to 55°F and the humidity was low. But, if you're Karolina Szabo and you've been given a free room, transportation and a good shot at winning $15,000 for first place, you can't exactly sit out the race in your air-conditioned hotel room eating beer nuts. For elite runners, racing—and training—in the heat is a fact of life.

Most elites do, however, take steps to ready themselves for the heat, and other runners can learn from their example. But before we get to those steps, let's look at how heat affects the body.

How Your Body Releases Heat

The body generates heat through metabolism, using food to create energy for the body. If you're sitting in front of the television, for example, the heat produced by your body hits about 98.6°F. But if you get off that couch and begin to run, heat from working muscles adds to the heat produced by your metabolism, driving up body temperature. Then, in an effort to return to normal, your body begins to sweat.

Perspiration and evaporation are the primary means for getting rid of excess heat and keeping the body cool. As warm blood is brought closer to the surface of the skin, the evaporating sweat cools the skin surface, which also cools the blood itself. The cooled blood then returns to the hot working muscles to control the rise in tissue temperature.

That's how your body works to keep from overheating. Of tremendous help in this cooling process is an important variable—fluids. The more you sweat, the more fluid you lose. In order to compensate for this, your body takes fluid from your blood (plasma) and moves it into the spaces around dehydrated tissues.

But this action reduces the amount of blood in your body, placing a strain on the circulatory system. The heart begins to beat faster, because there's less blood to go around and working muscles are screaming for blood to deliver nutrients and oxygen. Body temperature climbs because of less blood to cool muscles. Heat cramps, heat exhaustion and even heatstroke may result.

All this occurs not because the body can't handle the heat, but because it can't compensate for the fluid loss. It's dehydrated. Of course these problems are more likely to occur in hot, humid, stagnant weather, but dehydration can occur in weather as mild as 60°F and in cold winter temperatures as well.

Adjusting to the Heat

The good news is that just as the body adapts to altitude, it can also adjust to heat and humidity. Training in hot, humid conditions for one to two weeks increases your heat tolerance. A run you struggled through two weeks ago—in 80°F heat and 50 percent humidity—will now be less of a problem if your body is used to the heat. (During this adjustment period, though, you should run conservatively—a little slower and not to exhaustion—to avoid possible heat illness.)

As your body adjusts to the heat, several changes take place.

1. Profuse sweating allows more effective cooling. (Instead of beads of sweat on your forehead, you're sweating buckets around your neck, across your chest, down your arms and behind your knees.)
2. Sweat is diluted to conserve body minerals. (More of your sweat is just plain water.)

3. You sweat sooner and more freely. (The gun goes off and you're already dripping.)
4. Body temperature drops. (You're able to maintain 99°F instead of jumping to 101°.)
5. Heart rate decreases while doing the same amount of work. (The run you took two weeks ago doesn't seem as hard.)

What's to Drink?

Back in the 1960s, elite marathon runners drank defizzed colas and cold chicken soup during competitions. Sports drinks hadn't even been invented yet. Water and homemade concoctions had to go a long way.

Water is of course the best choice for any exercise lasting less than an hour. For distance runs, however, you're depleting the body of more than just water, so more must be replenished.

HEAT INJURY: KNOW THE SIGNS

Even heat-acclimated runners need to be wary of heat injuries, which progress through three stages: (1) heat cramps, (2) heat exhaustion and (3) heatstroke.

Heat cramps, usually affecting the leg muscles, are the most common and least serious of the three. Caused by a loss of minerals (sodium and potassium) through intense sweating, heat cramps can be remedied by stopping and replenishing these minerals by eating food, such as a banana, or gulping down an electrolyte-replacement drink like Gatorade.

Weakness, dizziness, goosebumps on your upper arms or chest, increased breathing and a rapid heart rate are all signs of heat exhaustion. You're seriously dehydrated at this stage, and your cardiovascular system is stressed to its limit. If you experience heat exhaustion, you need to stop, sit down in a shaded spot and drink lots of fluids immediately, or it can lead to phase three.

In heatstroke, the most serious stage, your body actually stops sweating, driving your temperature way up. Confusion, slurred speech and loss of consciousness may follow. At this point the body must be cooled immediately to protect against tissue damage or possibly death. Persons who have survived heatstroke are usually more prone to future heat injury, because they've altered their thermoregulatory mechanism and it may take time to regain heat tolerance.

Today there seem to be as many sports drinks on the shelf as soft drinks. This can make deciding what to drink a bit confusing. Ask a roomful of elite runners what they drink and they might each have a different answer—and every choice might be correct.

A good fluid replacement drink must offer two things: (1) It's easy to drink—in other words, it tastes good and it doesn't cause stomach cramps. (2) It empties out of the stomach fast, delivering fluid and nutrients to working muscles.

Do Sports Drinks Really Help?

Gatorade, Powerade, Hydrafuel, Ultrafuel...?

Rarely does a day go by when we aren't confronted with a magazine ad, a TV commercial or a billboard touting a sports drink. But wise runners know what is best for them and are not influenced by slick marketing, because the truth of the matter is: All sports drinks contain basically the same kinds of ingredients.

DRINKING ON THE RUN: TEN HOT TIPS

For safer running in the heat, most elites follow this advice.

1. Drink fluids (10 to 16 ounces) prior to all workouts.
2. Choose drinks low in sugar content (less than 8 percent).
3. Choose cold (45° to 55°F) drinks when possible; they are absorbed more quickly. Use ice cubes or pre-freeze partially filled water bottles.
4. Drink early and often (every 10 to 15 minutes or every aid station) during long runs or races.
5. Experiment with your tolerance for specific sports drinks in practice, not during competition.
6. Drink plenty of fluids, beyond your thirst, after running in the heat.
7. Weigh yourself often before and after training and racing in the heat to detect chronic dehydration. If you're down a pound or two, drink! Remember, one pint equals one pound.
8. Acclimatize yourself to the heat at least two weeks before long races.
9. Know the signs of heat injury.
10. Listen to your body and be smart. Don't ignore mild dizziness, fatigue or headache, which are all early signs of dehydration.

TIPS FROM THE TOP

Running in the Heat

Anne Marie Lauck, member of the 1995 U.S. World Track and Field Championships team at 10,000 meters: Elite road racer Anne Marie Lauck is a native of New Jersey, yet she has a history of running well in hot weather races like the Peachtree Road Race in Atlanta on the Fourth of July. Lauck was second in 1993 and first (31:57) in 1994, more than 30 seconds up on second and third place—two women runners from the hot-weather country of Kenya. Her secret?

"I take a sauna every day. That helps me be prepared year-round for racing in hot weather."

Joy Smith, 2:34 marathoner: "Living and training in Houston has taught me many lessons about the heat: Drink plenty of fluids before, during and after all training runs. That is a given and can't be stressed too much. But I've also learned that training in the heat is a lot like altitude training. My times for intervals and the volume of miles must be adjusted. I don't run as fast or recover as quickly when the temperature is 95°F and the humididty is 90 percent. When days like that crop up, I sometimes head for the pool and do some water running, or I go inside and run on a treadmill—or I head for a cooler, drier climate!"

Steve Spence, 1991 World Marathon Championships bronze medalist and a 1992 Olympic marathoner: When Spence won the bronze at the 1991 World Championships in Tokyo, the day was hot and humid.

"The main key is that you don't need to train in miserable conditions to get used to running in the heat. If you pull sweats on and jump in a sauna to run, you're just going to tear your body down and destroy yourself. I think running around Pennsylvania in the summer is plenty hot to get used to the heat. In Tokyo it was 86°F with 80 percent humidity.

"When running in the heat, you just have to remember to hydrate well before, during and also afterward. When I go on my 20-milers in the summer, I drink before and after, and either I have someone ride along on a bike with me to give me water during the run or, if I'm alone, I'll pick out a four-mile loop and set water bottles out so that I get water every four miles. It gets a little boring running the same loop five times, but getting fluids is more important than keeping yourself entertained."

- Water, for hydration
- Carbohydrates in the form of simple sugars (glucose, sucrose or fructose), for energy
- Electrolytes (sodium, potassium, chloride and phosphorus), to replace those minerals lost during running

Do they work? Today's research indicates that sports drinks may indeed be more effective than water. Sodium and carbohydrates can increase fluid absorption because sodium is readily absorbed in the small intestines; thus, these drinks are more likely to enter the system than water alone, which would end up in the bladder. Solutions containing sodium may also reduce the risk of electrolyte imbal-

RACING STRATEGIES FOR HOT WEATHER

It's 88°F at the starting line of the aptly named Utica Boilermaker 15-K in Utica, New York. What are some elites thinking about—besides an air-conditioned room and a cold drink?

Jill Hunter, two-time British Olympian (3000 meters in 1988 and 10,000 meters in 1992): "I'm telling myself I'm glad I didn't wear black. Light clothing is a must in hot weather racing."

Don Janicki, 2:11 marathoner: "I'm telling myself to stay hydrated—this means I take all fluids that I can, not just at the fluid stations but from anyone out on the course with a cup of water. Also, to stay cool—figuratively—and not run stupid. I also remind myself that it's hot, so I shouldn't worry about my finishing time, just about giving a solid effort."

Debbi Kilpatrick-Morris, winner of the 1995 U.S. National Marathon Championships: "I tend to run conservative races in any weather, so I'm telling myself that my conservative strategy will work today. I'm careful to drink a lot early in the race—that's the most crucial time to drink in a marathon. If you're thirsty late in a race, it's sometimes too late. And I'm also telling myself to relax."

Annette Peters, 1992 U.S. Olympian at 3000 meters: "I work on staying relaxed and not getting mentally stressed about the heat, because everyone in the race has to face the same heat and humidity."

Ric Sayre, 1983 Los Angeles Marathon winner and elite masters runner: "I'm reminding myself to start out slow because you really can suffer from going out too fast in the heat."

TYPICAL TRAINING SCHEDULE FOR JOY SMITH

In summer the heat in Texas can be devastating for runners. Joy Smith, a 2:34 marathoner, has found that frequent fluids and a slower pace help her workouts. In heavy heat she switches to poolwork, doing water running instead.

Sunday	A.M.	22 mi. on trails
Monday	A.M.	6 mi., 7:00 pace
	P.M.	18 min. warm-up; 4 × 1 mi. (5:12–5:16 pace); 15 min. cooldown
Tuesday	A.M.	4 mi. (7:00 pace or equivalent) in pool (during high heat)
	P.M.	12 mi., with 2 × 6 min. pickups (5:30 pace)
Wednesday	A.M.	6 mi., 7:00 pace
	P.M.	18 min. warm-up; 4 × 400 m. (70–72 sec.), with 30 sec. rest interval; 15 min. cooldown
Thursday	A.M.	9 mi. (7:00 pace or equivalent) in pool (during high heat)
Friday	A.M.	Recovery day; 30 min., easy
Saturday	A.M.	10 mi., 6:30 pace

ance, a rare but potentially dangerous condition for runners. In addition, the carbohydrates in sports drinks serve as an energy source during long runs and can help prevent blood sugar levels from dropping.

So for strenuous, long workouts, the benefits of drinking the right sports drink can exceed the benefits of drinking just plain water. Yet, as many runners have discovered, some sports drinks can cause abdominal cramping for some people. Much depends on the individual and on the type of sugar used. Often, drinks that are high in fructose are absorbed more slowly and may be more likely to cause cramping.

Try out a sports drink like you would try out a new pair of shoes. Give it a test run in practice, and take the time to get used to it before depending on it in a race. If you're still wary of stomach distress, stick with water.

When and How Much?

"Hydrate, hydrate, hydrate," Lynn Jennings, the 1992 Olympic 10,000 meters bronze medalist, says when asked what to do about running in hot weather. That means drinking before *and* during any race or training session—and afterward as well. It's not unusual for a runner to lose as much as one liter of water per hour through sweat. For your best performance you need to replace as much as possible.

Brad Hudson, 1992 and 1993 Columbus Marathon winner, downs about 12 ounces of a sports drink just minutes before the start of any marathon. This ensures that he's properly hydrated at the beginning of the race, and that's half the battle. But watch that you don't drink too much—and get waterlogged and bloated. You don't want to slosh when you run—or wait in line for a port-a-john at the five-mile mark.

Once the race begins, when you drink—even for most elite runners—is in the hands of the race director. Races held in hot weather usually provide fluid every couple of miles. Most elites take advantage of every fluid station, especially early on, grabbing one or two cups and drinking as much as possible.

One secret that all elite runners learn with experience is to squeeze the top of the paper cup together, leaving a small opening. Drinking from a smaller opening is easier and you're less likely to spill. Drink three to six ounces every 10 to 15 minutes or at every opportunity.

The same care you take in drinking during a race should carry over to a long run in practice. Elites like Steve Spence set out water bottles at certain mile marks or plan routes around park water fountains in the summer. If you run in a large city, tuck a dollar in your pocket and buy a bottle of water at the neighborhood deli.

One of the most important times to drink is after a race or workout. "Take plenty of fluids before, during and especially after your run—when your fluid level is the lowest," says Laurie Gomez-Henes, member of the 1995 U.S. World Track and Field Championships team at 10,000 meters. To avoid chronic dehydration—walking around with a low fluid tank that your body, through time, interprets as normal—drink beyond your thirst following every race or hard workout.

Training and Racing in the Cold

With a half-mile left in the 1989 Pittsburgh Marathon, the temperature had dropped and snow was falling. Ken Martin and John Tuttle were locked in a battle for first, no doubt planning when and where to kick. But as they entered Point State Park for the finish, Tuttle, a native of Georgia, made a wrong turn. Martin accelerated and won by a few seconds—2:15:28 to 2:15:33. Afterward, Tuttle, teeth chattering and lips as blue as a robin's egg, said he lost his concentration for a second because of the cold, and that's why he made a wrong turn. A $7,000 wrong turn—the difference between the prize money for first and second.

Cold weather! Snow. Ice. Cold fingers and toes. Frozen eyelashes and nose hairs. Blue lips. Just the thought makes many elite runners want to pull up next to a warm fire and wait until April. Fortunately, that thought quickly passes, and they bundle up and head out the door.

And that's a good decision, because despite its bad reputation, running in the cold presents fewer problems than running in the heat. "All you need to do is wear proper clothing," says New Hampshire runner Cathy O'Brien. "Other than that, cold weather is really not a problem."

Running in a Deep Freeze

Just as your body responds to heat by sweating, it protects itself from cold as well. Let's see what the cold actually does to runners.

On a winter morning you step out the door, see your breath and

TIPS FROM THE TOP

COLD-WEATHER RUNNING

Debbi Kilpatrick-Morris, winner of the 1995 U.S. National Marathon Championships: Debbi Kilpatrick-Morris trains year-round in Cleveland, where arctic winds sometimes come across Lake Erie like a precursor to another ice age.

"I've run in the winter where the windchill is 20° to 30°F below zero! If it gets any colder than that I run inside, because after a certain point my ski mask freezes. I also know when to stay inside. If I have to bundle up to extremes just to get out the door, I run on a treadmill. You can't put six layers on and go for a run.

"In truly cold weather two keys for me are keeping my feet warm and drinking a lot of water. In the past couple of years I've found that the shoes I wear on a run make a big difference. Today, some of the lighter-weight shoes made of nylon just don't keep my feet warm enough. That's why I'll go with a heavier shoe—preferably one that has leather around the toe box—when I'm running in the cold.

"I also put out water—or have routine water stops—even on short runs in the cold. Dehydration is a serious problem because most people feel they don't need as much water when it's cold. The thirst is not as acute as it is in hot weather, so they tend not to drink—and then they run into problems. I leave bottles of water in my car so that at certain times, say at the 3-, 6- and 9-mile points of a 12-mile run, I'll double back to the car and take a drink. Otherwise, I find myself not thinking about it, and before long I'm dehydrated."

Anne Marie Lauck, member of the 1995 U.S. World Track and Field Championships team at 10,000 meters: "In cold weather I prefer to be a little overdressed rather than underdressed—if I'm cold, I could end up pulling a muscle because the muscle is not as limber. It's important to me to keep my legs warm."

Sonia O'Sullivan, 1992 Irish Olympian at 3000 meters: "If it's difficult to drink cold water after a run in the cold, drink hot water with a lemon slice or herbal decaffeinated teas."

Ken Popejoy, world masters champ at 1500 meters in 1991 and 1993: "Training in the cold requires proper selection of clothing—no heavy, bulky nylon materials. Make sure you have warm clothing on your torso and arms but only minimal layers on your legs."

feel the cold. As you stand there, your body adjusts to the cold by conserving heat loss. It does so by constricting blood vessels near the surface of exposed skin to let less heat out. As you become colder, your body also increases heat production by adding movement—little uncontrollable shakes of the body known as shivers.

Then you begin to run. As you run, blood is circulated to working muscles, which begin to generate heat. Plus, the movement of running replaces the need to shiver, adding to body warmth. In fact, racing in cool conditions usually produces better performances than racing in hot weather because the reduced blood flow to the skin allows for greater blood flow to the working muscles that need extra energy.

As long as it's not too severe, cold weather is ideal for distance running. The cooler weather keeps the body from overheating. If body temperature drops below normal (hypothermia), however, aerobic capacity decreases, which will affect endurance and performance. This decrease in aerobic power is caused by lower maximal heart rate and cardiac output (blood pumped by the heart each minute). Let's look at what happens if the body is unable to compensate for exposure to the cold.

Exposure: What Can Go Wrong

It's the million-dollar question everybody asks: Won't I freeze my lungs if I try to run in cold temperature? The answer is simple: No. The fact is, even in severely cold weather the air you breathe is warmed to about the same temperature as the body when it passes through the upper respiratory area (nostrils, mouth and throat). Your rapid breathing during exercise in the cold may produce some throat irritation, but it will not freeze the tissues in the throat and lungs.

Hypothermia—the dropping of the body's core temperature below 95°F that Tuttle experienced in its initial stages—is a potential problem when running in the cold. The risk of hypothermia (which can be fatal if the core temperature drops below 78°F) is greatly increased by high humidity and wearing wet clothing. Even in relatively mild conditions—say, 53°F—once you slow down or stop you begin to lose heat rapidly. So it's not a good idea to stand around too long at the finish line after a race.

Early signs of hypothermia include fatigue and cloudy thinking. As body temperature drops, heart rate and respiration are lowered, and a runner may stagger or find concentration more difficult. He will start to shiver. Eventually, if pushed to exhaustion, he may fall or pass out. Results may be disastrous in situations where he is running by himself on a quiet road or trail and no one else is around.

We associate frostbite with long exposure to severe cold, but the truth is your extremities can become frostbitten rather quickly—within 60 seconds when the wind is strong or hypothermia has reduced body temperature below normal.

Your extremities account for 50 percent of body surface area, so a great deal of your body is at risk. Decreased blood flow to your fingers and toes means your body is saving warmth for its vital organs. When blood is pulled to the body core, the combination of internal cooling and outside exposure can cause the water within the extremities to freeze. Ice crystals form between the cells, further cutting off blood flow.

The signs of frostbite are progressive: feeling cold, then numb, and finally warm. The skin first appears blue, then whitish or gray spots may appear, and swelling may follow.

To treat the frostbitten area, hold the exposed part against your torso for warmth or immerse the part in warm water. Do not rub the area, as tissues are easily damaged. Never give alcohol, as it dilates the blood vessels and carries the cold to the body's core.

After the frostbite thaws, bandage the area to protect it against rubbing or other damage. Do not go outside again without adequate protection, as refreezing can irreparably damage the area. In the future, protect these areas; frostbite is more likely to recur in areas previously frostbitten. At greatest risk are those who are wet, who have become exhausted, who have recently drunk alcohol or who have had frostbite before.

Both hypothermia and frostbite can easily be combated if you dress appropriately and don't take risks.

Wind: Is It a Factor?

The wind is sort of a wild card in cold-weather running. Temperatures in the 50s—not bad for a long, easy 12-miler—can actually feel like the 30s when the wind's blowing 14 miles per hour. Your body loses heat in the wind as air currents strip energy from your body's surface. Runners who make the mistake of wearing shorts and a singlet on cool days open themselves up to hypothermia and frostbite when the wind begins to blow. So before running in the cold, consult the "Windchill Chart" to know how to dress for the conditions.

And on windy days, take advice from 1992 British Olympic marathoner Steve Brace, who recommends running "into the wind on the way out, and with the wind at your back on your return." That way, the cooling effect of the wind will hit you early—when your body is generating sufficient heat—not later in the run when you're thinking about your down comforter and a cup of hot cocoa.

WINDCHILL CHART

WIND SPEED (MPH)	THERMOMETER READING (°F)							
	50	**40**	**30**	**20**	**10**	**0**	**-10**	**-20**
Calm	50	40	30	20	10	0	-10	-20
5	48	37	27	16	6	-5	-15	-26
10	40	28	16	4	-9	-24	-33	-46
15	36	22	9	-5	-18	-32	-45	-58
20	32	18	4	-10	-25	-39	-52	-67
25	30	16	0	-15	-29	-44	-59	-74
30	28	13	-2	-18	-33	-48	-63	-79
35	27	11	-4	-20	-35	-51	-67	-82
40	26	10	-6	-21	-37	-53	-69	-85

LITTLE DANGER (for properly clothed person)

INCREASING DANGER (exposed flesh may freeze)

GREAT DANGER (flesh may freeze within 3 min.)

Feeling the Cold: It's All Relative

"Hey! She's not even wearing tights!" At the 1989 Pittsburgh Marathon Margaret Groos won the women's division—running 2:32:58 through snowflakes in a thin, one-piece running outfit that exposed her arms and legs. Back in third, New Zealand's Erin Baker (2:36:58) wore a bodysuit covering her from head to toe.

Some people seem to tolerate the cold better than others. Why? Some of it is simply attitude—and what you're used to. In other words, if you simply don't consider temperatures above freezing very cold, you may run comfortably in 36°F weather. Also, if you've run through most of the winter in temperatures below zero, you're not likely to find 36° in March very cold by comparison.

Besides the mind-set, though, three physical factors play a role in how we retain body heat: body surface area, body fat and age.

Body surface area. The amount of heat needed to maintain normal body temperature is directly related to surface area (where

RULES OF THE COLD

Cold-weather running can be fun and may even produce personal records, but to quote Dirty Harry, "A man must know his limitations." To run smart, most elite runners follow these guidelines for comfortable and safe winter running.

1. Always consult a windchill chart on windy days and use the equivalent temperature for determining what to wear.
2. Dress in several layers of light outerwear instead of one heavy layer. Avoid tight socks and gloves, which can hamper circulation.
3. Avoid running into a head wind whenever possible.
4. Wear a hat and gloves to avoid heat loss and frostbite.
5. Don't overdress on moderately cool days.
6. Avoid excessive skin exposure in severe cold.
7. Avoid standing around after competition on cold days.
8. Exercise indoors on extremely cold days, or at least warm up and cool down indoors.
9. Warm up for a longer period before running a fast pace.
10. Drink plenty of fluids before, during and after hard runs on cold days. You may not feel as thirsty because of the cold, but your body loses a lot of fluid.
11. Use common sense. Don't take chances. If possible, run with a partner.

heat escapes). Since runners tend to be smaller than average, you'd think they have an advantage in the cold over, say, linebackers and sumo wrestlers. The truth is, when you consider the ratio of body surface area to body weight, the smaller person has to produce more energy to maintain his body temperature compared with someone larger.

Body fat. Fat serves as a good insulator against the cold. Obviously, lean, leggy runners are at a disadvantage here. But what about women, who naturally have more body fat than men? Can they tolerate the cold better? The answer is no. That's because women are usually smaller and have less muscle mass and a lower aerobic capacity (the heat-making capacity) than men. When these facts are considered, there seems to be little difference between the sexes. Carl and Cathy will get cold at the same rate.

Age. As we get older, we seem to lose our tolerance for cold. Young adults—who can generate more heat because they have a more efficient aerobic engine—are usually not bothered by the cold as much as their mothers and fathers. Older runners therefore should not gauge their dress for a race by watching the younger elite runners prance around in singlets and shorts when it's 34°F out and they're shivering in tights and windbreakers. If you're cold, put on another layer.

Dress Like an Onion

It's no secret: Running in the cold can be a day at the beach "if you wear enough clothing and it's the right kind," says Steve Spence, the 1991 World Marathon Championships bronze medalist and a 1992 Olympic marathoner. With today's new styles and lightweight materials—such as polypropylene, cotton mesh or GoreTex (which is waterproof and breathable)—running clothes are warmer and more comfortable than the old baggy cotton sweats that soaked up 20 pounds of rain, snow or sweat and stretched six inches after running.

Even with all the high-tech fabrics, some runners tend to overdress, and thus may suffer from overheating and dehydration during a long run or a race. They want to be warm while standing on the starting line, and think they have to finish the race wearing what they started with.

"The secret to handling the cold is to dress in disposable layers," says Ric Sayre, an elite masters runner. "I dress to be comfortable at the start of each run, and as I become overheated, I just peel off a layer and continue." Be careful, however, not to take too much off at

FITS LIKE A GLOVE

Some elite runners, like Mexico's Salvador Garcia, wear gloves in cool—not just cold—weather. At the 1991 New York City Marathon, Garcia won the race wearing white gloves, even though temperatures were in the 50s and 60s.

Why the gloves? One reason is comfort; Garcia doesn't like cool hands. But another reason has to do with performance. By keeping his hands warm, Garcia was ensuring that all needed blood would be sent to the working muscles in his legs instead of to his cold hands. By creating a micro-environment with the gloves, the fingers stayed warm and blood was shunted to the working muscles instead of warming the fingers.

TYPICAL TRAINING SCHEDULE FOR DEBBI KILPATRICK-MORRIS

Living in Cleveland, Debbi Kilpatrick-Morris, winner of the 1995 U.S. National Marathon Championships, runs regularly in the winter in temperatures far below zero. Her shoes are heavier models with leather for added protection against the cold, and for longer runs she plans water stops along the way.

Sunday		45 min. (7:00 pace)
Monday		45 min. (7:00 pace)
Tuesday	A.M.	40 min. (6:30 pace), indoors if very cold
	P.M.	20 min. warm-up; alternating 4 × 800 m. (2:35), 400 m. (72 sec.) with 400 m. recovery jogs; 20 min. cooldown
Wednesday		45 min. (7:00 pace), indoors if very cold
Thursday	A.M.	40 min. (6:30 pace)
	P.M.	20 min. warm-up; 6 × 5 min. (5:35–5:40 pace) with 2 min. recovery jogs; 20 min. cooldown
Friday		45 min. (7:00 pace)
Saturday	A.M.	Long run for 2:40, leaving water bottles in car parked along bike trail
	P.M.	40 min. (6:30 pace)

once, which could cause rapid cooling. Once you have a chill, it's almost too late to put clothes back on again—not only because you've already lost precious body heat but also because more often than not your sweatshirt is two miles back at the car where you left it!

Each layer you wear should wick moisture away from the body; wearing wet clothes can chill a runner quickly. Wear polypropylene as a first layer, closest to the body, to pull moisture away from the skin.

Also, as Reuben Reina reminds us, "Don't forget to wear your hat and gloves." Sounds like Mom talking, but it's true. Even though your head represents only about 7 to 9 percent of your body surface area, your body can lose significant heat through the top of your head. Think of your head as a smokestack: Left uncovered, all the heat goes out the top.

Gloves are important, too, even in moderate weather. As the energy needs by the muscles increase, blood flow is diminished in the extremities, such as the hands, leaving them susceptible to frostbite. At major races elites often wear thin gloves—there are the loose, white cotton painter's gloves made popular by Bill Rodgers, four-time winner of the Boston Marathon, and the newer snug polypropylene ones—taking them off and tucking them in their shorts when their hands are comfortable, then putting them back on later if their hands get cold.

CHAPTER

15

The Effects of Altitude

LESS OXYGEN MEANS MORE WORK

When Jim Ryun looked up with 100 meters to go in the 1968 Olympic 1500 meter final, he saw Kenya's Kip Keino far ahead and on his way to winning the gold medal.

What onlookers saw was an altitude-trained athlete (Keino) beating one who trained near sea level (Ryun).

Since the late 1960s, with the emergence of Kenya's great distance runners who live and train at altitude, the question of altitude training has intrigued everyone—especially elite athletes. Indeed, this lure has created running meccas in some parts of the country. Boulder, Colorado, for example, at 6,000 feet, has long been home to distance-running greats such as Frank Shorter and Arturo Barrios. But the question remains: Does altitude training really help? For every elite runner who says yes, there's another who says no. So before we get into this debate, let's look at what we know about the effects of altitude on performance and training.

Rocky Mountain High?

When competing at altitude in events lasting longer than a couple of minutes, running will be more difficult and produce slower times than at sea level. So why would anyone want to train there? Many runners believe that the increased stress of running in the thinner air will allow you to get more out of your mileage.

How? you ask. Let's look at what happens when you head for the mountains.

As you go from sea level to altitude, the air pressure lessens. This decrease in air pressure lowers the oxygen density, which means there is less oxygen in each breath. You then need to breathe deeper or faster to get the same amount of oxygen you would get into your lungs at sea level.

MOVING UP IN THE WORLD

Elite runners who do spend time at altitude heed these training tips.

1. Train at moderate altitude (6,500 to 7,500 feet).
2. Spend at least two to four weeks at altitude, with intermittent trips to lower elevations to work on leg speed and power. It may take several months to become completely adjusted.
3. To avoid dehydration, drink plenty of fluids.
4. Schedule competitions at sea level within a few days after arrival there.
5. Avoid alcohol! A beer at 8,000 feet is like three at sea level.
6. Reduce training to avoid overtraining.
7. Expect less benefit if you're already well-conditioned.

The lower air pressure cuts into your aerobic capacity—that is, your ability to produce energy on the run. This reduced oxygen consumption affects endurance events dramatically. These side effects aren't noticeable until about 5,000 feet; after that, though, for every 1,000 feet climbed maximal aerobic capacity is cut by about 3 to 3.5 percent. So if you race at altitude keeping the same pace you're accustomed to at sea level, you have to run at a higher percentage of your capacity because you can't get as much oxygen. And since racing requires about 85 to 90 percent of your aerobic capacity, maintaining the same pace at altitude is virtually impossible. You have to slow down.

What does this mean in a race? Suppose you can run a 36-minute 10-K in Cleveland, Ohio, which is only a few feet above sea level. Then you go to Boulder, Colorado, and run that 10-K at about 6,000 feet. Because you lose about 3.5 percent of your aerobic capacity, the same effort will have you shaking your head and staring at 37 minutes and some change as you cross the line.

By the way, sprinting is not affected to a great extent by altitude. These events take only a few seconds, and the demands on the oxygen transport system are minimal. This was obvious during the 1968 Olympics in Mexico City, which took place at 7,300 feet. Sprinters ran about the same times as at sea level, while distance runners ran slower times than usual to win their races.

TIPS FROM THE TOP

ALTITUDE TRAINING

Don Janicki, 2:11 marathoner: "I've been living and training at altitude for five years, and I think that it has definitely extended my marathon career. The thing is, at altitude the running I'm doing to get a hard cardiovascular workout is not as structurally hard on my body as at sea level. That's because you don't have to run as fast—pound as hard—to get the same benefits. And with less pounding comes a longer marathon career."

Jon Sinclair, two-time U.S. Olympic Marathon Trials qualifier (1988 and 1992): "I've lived all of my adult life at altitude—5,000 feet in Fort Collins, Colorado—although I think you have to be a bit higher, probably 7,000 feet, to get the full effect of altitude training.

"I can remember in my early years always feeling really bad at the beginning of races. The gun would go off and I would struggle to keep up with the leaders. After a while I'd settle down and be comfortable, but the early going, when the pace tended to be faster, was always a chore. That was because my workouts at altitude were slower than those of runners who ran at sea level. I just didn't have the turnover they did. I suffered from lack of speed.

"Then, too, we pay a price for training up here because it slows down your interval training, which decreases leg speed. So when I do, say, 20 × 400 meters at altitude, I'll be doing well to do them in 66 to 67 seconds. At sea level I would run them in 64 to 65 seconds. If you draw out the analogy the whole way, that means all of your workouts are going to be slower at altitude. And that, of course, causes problems when it's time to race fast.

"Yet I've found some benefits as well. In my college days I ran races back to back on a single afternoon. I noticed that I

How Your Body Adapts

As a "flatlander," when you travel from sea level to altitude, you'll notice the change right away. Climbing a flight of steps will leave you panting for breath, your heart pounding. In this thinner air your body works harder to deliver oxygen to the muscles.

The rapid breathing (hyperventilation) increases the oxygen level in the lungs. At the same time, however, you're also blowing off more carbon dioxide than normal. Losing more carbon dioxide from blood tended to recover more quickly. And when I jumped into road racing, I found that at the top of really steep hills, when everyone was blown out, oftentimes I'd recover sooner. And that's because at home I'd had to deal with lower oxygen problems all the time.

"Ultimately, the best situation would be to do your aerobic work in the mountains, then come back down to sea level for your speedwork. If you could find a place in the mountains that's an hour drive from sea level, you could spend most of the week up there doing your aerobic work, then once or twice a week get in your car and drive to the track for speedwork at sea level. You'd have the best of both worlds."

Steve Spence, 1991 World Marathon Championships bronze medalist and a 1992 Olympic marathoner: "Depending on what you're doing, altitude training can either help you or hurt you. If you're doing easy mileage and trying to build a big base it can help you get strong—if you can go to altitude and run the same number of miles without breaking down. But going to altitude hurts when you're trying to get ready for a race. Speedwork is much more difficult. When I'm at altitude, I need to either slow down my repeats or increase the rest interval, or both.

"I remember the first time I went to altitude. It was very hard for me to adapt; it took a long time—almost three weeks—before my body started feeling normal. I had heavy legs and felt tired all the time. Finally, I felt better, and what I really learned about altitude is that you have to compromise. You have to know your limitations because you can't go up there and do the same workouts you did at sea level without breaking yourself down. It just can't be done."

disrupts your acid-base balance, so until you become acclimatized you are losing some of your natural buffers against buildup of lactic acid, a by-product of exertion as oxygen is depleted. That's why your legs feel like lead when you run at altitude, at least during the first few days.

Furthermore, your jackhammer-in-love heart rate causes problems, too. An increased heart rate is needed to deliver oxygen to the tissues, but you then have less heart rate reserve for exercise, resulting in higher heart rates for training efforts—even easy ones. So you're working harder all the time, even when you're going slow.

Finally, the thin, dry air makes a runner more prone to dehydration than at sea level. You lose water much faster through respiration and evaporation. Even mild dehydration adds to fatigue and slower times.

With these changes, you're probably wondering why anyone would want to train at altitude. The answer lies in one long-term effect: Over time the body increases its production of red blood cells, which contain hemoglobin the transporter of oxygen in the blood. With more hemoglobin the runner adapts to the thinner air and suffers less from breathlessness and rapid heart rate. This increase in red blood cells remains for several days after leaving altitude, and this, many speculate, is the secret of runners who live and train at altitude and race at sea level.

Indeed, many elite runners, such as 10-K world-record holder Yobes Ondieki (who trains in New Mexico), will stay at altitude until the last possible moment before traveling to a sea-level race such as the Revco/Cleveland 10-K, since the increase in hemoglobin and red blood cells, increasing the blood's capacity for carrying oxygen, lasts only a few days.

With the changes that occur in altitude training, you would think that performance upon return to sea level would be better; research does not bear this out, however. In the long run, the changes may not be worth the effort—especially when you take into account all that packing up and moving to altitude entails. "I'm not really into altitude training because it involves such a big move," says New Hampshire's Cathy O'Brien. "I prefer to stay where I am and run familiar courses— and have all the comforts of home."

Even when an elite athlete does move to altitude, it's not an instant panacea. Early in his career, Pennsylvania's Steve Spence packed up and went to Colorado for three straight summers. He found it took at least two to four weeks before he became acclimated. Finally, unless an elite has a summer home in Boulder—or a lot of spare change—the expense of training at altitude may be another reason for staying at home and simply training harder. Indeed, many world-class runnners, such as Lynn Jennings (who lives in New Hampshire) and Bob Kennedy (who lives in Indiana), have never trained at altitude.

Should You Head for the Mountains?

The argument about altitude training is still not settled. Even Jon Sinclair, a two-time U.S. Olympic Marathon Trials qualifier who lives at 5,000 feet in Fort Collins, Colorado, is not convinced. "I'm not sure there is much benefit in altitude training," he says. The fact of the matter is, though the body goes through some major adaptations at alti-

FEELING LOW AS YOU GO UP

As you travel to high elevations, from 5,000 to over 10,000 feet, more than the view can leave you reeling. Altitude sickness is very unpredictable and can affect anyone. It may strike someone who is in good health and highly fit, while someone less fit will be unaffected. The most common symptoms, from mild to severe, are listed here.

- Listlessness, drowsiness, dizziness
- Fainting
- Severe headache, extreme thirst
- Sleep disturbances
- Appetite loss, weakness, slower reflexes
- Nausea, vomiting
- Heart palpitations, pounding pulse
- Congested lungs, difficulty in breathing

To lessen the severity of altitude sickness, ascend gradually and rest when you first arrive at higher elevations. Rest at least 24 hours when traveling to 9,000 feet, and 48 hours if you go to 12,000 feet or above. If you can, to avoid sleep disturbances, return to lower elevations (below 8,000 feet) for sleeping. Because dehydration will add to your fatigue and headache, drink plenty of fluids and avoid alcohol. Drink more than you need to quench thirst.

tude—which would seem beneficial to the athlete upon return to sea level—not many studies shout "Altitude training will make you faster!" So why, then, are elite runners still scurrying off to train at altitude? Boulder in the summer, for example, looks like the Olympic village for elite runners.

One reason is that altitude training gives us more from our mileage with less wear and tear on our bodies. Why? Because the effort to run 6:30 pace at 6,000 feet is equal to the effort necessary to run 6:00 pace at sea level. That means we don't have to put our legs through 6:00 pace to get a 6:00-pace workout for our heart and lungs. But there's a downside. A slower pace may alter our running mechanics, decreasing muscle power and leg turnover. These changes could make us less efficient when we race at lower altitudes. The two, it seems, cancel each other out.

One thing is certain: Altitude training gives you the edge *if you plan to race at altitude*—remember, the Mexico City Games were at an altitude of 7,300 feet. Yet even this is not as simple as it sounds. An

TYPICAL TRAINING SCHEDULE FOR JON SINCLAIR

Two-time U.S. Olympic Marathon Trials qualifier Jon Sinclair trains at 5,000 feet in Fort Collins, Colorado. He includes three days of speed training to avoid slow leg turnover. Plus, he runs downhill to stimulate faster leg turnover.

Sunday	A.M.	1½ to 2½ hr. run
Monday	A.M.	5 mi., easy (6:30 pace)
	P.M.	5 mi., easy
Tuesday	A.M.	10 mi., steady (5:30–5:45 pace)
	P.M.	2 mi. warm-up; 14 × 200 m. (33–35 sec.), with 200 m. (jog) rest; 2 mi. cooldown
Wednesday	A.M.	10 mi., easy
	P.M.	5 mi., easy
Thursday	A.M.	12 mi. gradual uphill at 6:00 pace, then 3 mi. downhill at 5:10 pace
Friday	A.M.	10 mi., easy
	P.M.	5 mi., easy
Saturday	A.M.	2 mi. warm-up; 5 × 1000 m. (2:55), with 200 m. (jog) rest; 2 mi. cooldown
	P.M.	5 mi., easy

elite runner who wants to run well at, say, the Bolder Boulder 10-K has to figure out how long before the race he needs to go to altitude.

And how he can afford it.

High-*Attitude* Training: A Nice Place to Visit

The real reason many runners excel after training in places like Boulder may not be directly attributed to the altitude itself: "The company of other highly motivated runners can be very conducive to high-level training," says Jon Sinclair. "That's why you see so much success there."

In other words, you can never underestimate the psychological effects of beautiful mountain scenery and a populace that rallies around its runners. The true secret in running meccas like Boulder, then, may not be the altitude—instead, it might be the attitude these meccas inspire in runners.

CHAPTER

16

Nutrition

EATING TO RUN

Reindeer milk. Froot Loops. Cold pizza with mayonnaise. Turtle soup. Over the years, these are just a few of the foods that elite runners have (tongue-in-cheek and not) confessed to eating to help them get to the finish line faster.

But elite runners know that good nutrition is nothing to joke about. Most are very serious about what they eat every day, and even those who don't monitor their diets daily become very aware of what they eat as an important race draws near. A Wendy's chicken sandwich, a large order of fries and a Dr. Pepper might see U.S. Olympic steeplechaser Mark Croghan through a routine workout in January (yes, Croghan eats like this occasionally), but you can bet your bottom dollar that this meal isn't on Croghan's menu card the night before an Olympic final.

Training Diets: Energy to Run

During intense training elite runners sometimes consume as much as twice the calories each day as they normally would. How do they know if they're eating enough? Hunger is one indicator, but it's not infallible. The best gauge is the daily weigh-in: If they are steadily losing weight, they need to eat more.

A more difficult question is what to eat. If your body weight is steady, you're consuming enough calories—but are these calories supplying the right nutrients for top performance? According to the National Academy of Sciences, the Daily Value for energy nutrients is 20 to 30 percent fat, 58 to 70 percent carbohydrates, and 12 to 15 percent protein. Elite runners tend to require the higher values where carbohydrates and protein are concerned, and a proportionately lower number of calories from fat: 65 to 70 percent carbohydrates, around 15 percent protein and 15 to 20 percent fat.

Let's look briefly at each of the components of the elite runner's diet.

Carbohydrates: pasta party. For runners and nonrunners alike, the most important food energy source is carbohydrates, which are used by the body to replenish glycogen in muscle cells, to generate heat and to supply glucose for energy and to maintain metabolism. Carbohydrates come in two forms: simple carbohydrates (sugars) and complex carbohydrates (starches). Even though both types supply energy, complex carbohydrates are more nutrient dense (supply more nutrients per number of calories) than sugars. Therefore, most carbohydrates in the diet should be from complex carbohydrates (breads, potatoes) as opposed to sugars (sugary soft drinks).

Protein: Steak your claim. Your body uses protein for growth and repair of tissues, to produce hormones and as a source of energy when carbohydrates and fat are no longer available. For the average runner, from 12 to 15 percent of total calories should come from protein, which is usually not a problem with most training diets. Some research, however, indicates that runners may need more protein in the diet to repair tissue damage incurred during hard training or racing.

After the 1995 U.S. Men's Marathon Championships, for example, Ed Eyestone, second place in the race, sat down in the hotel restaurant to eat a hamburger for lunch. He wasn't alone; several other elite runners were also eating protein—chicken, fish, cheese—to help repair the muscle damage done to their legs from pounding 26.2 miles of pavement.

Yet eating several hamburgers—or any other form of protein, such as fish, chicken or dairy products—will not make you faster. In fact, it might do just the opposite. That's because excess protein, say more than 20 grams in a single meal, is stored by the body as fat.

Fats: energy for the long run. The most concentrated food energy comes in the form of fats, which pack over twice the calories per gram (nine) than protein or carbohydrates (four). In addition to providing energy during the later stages of a marathon or while running at a slow pace, fat is needed to store and transport fat-soluble vitamins throughout the body and to regulate hormone levels. Since many foods contain fat, runners usually don't have to worry about not getting enough fat in their diets, but do have to worry about getting too much: Excess calories from fat are stored in the body as excess fat.

Take Your Vitamins?

The body needs small amounts of vitamins for regulating metabolism—converting fats and carbohydrates to usable energy—and to as-

VITAMIN-RICH FOODS

NUTRIENT	DAILY VALUE	FOOD SOURCES
Vitamin A	5,000 IU	Milk, cheese, eggs, dark green leafy vegetables, carrots, sweet potatoes, yellow squash
Vitamin B-complex		Meat (beef, pork, poultry, fish), eggs, milk, cheese, beans, nuts, starchy vegetables, whole greens
Thiamin	1.5 mg.	
Riboflavin	1.7 mg.	
B_6	2 mg.	
B_{12}	6 mcg.	
Vitamin C	60 mg.	Fruits, vegetables
Vitamin D	400 IU	Fortified milk, cheese, eggs, salmon, tuna
Vitamin E	30 IU	Vegetable oils, green leafy vegetables, wheat germ, whole-grain cereals and breads
Vitamin K	*	Green leafy vegetables, cabbage, eggs, peas, potatoes, milk

*No Daily Value. The Recommended Daily Allowance is 65–80 mcg.

sist in producing strong bones and other tissues. Concern about vitamin deficiency may cause runners to look to supplements, most often the one-a-day, 100 percent across-the-board tablets. Olympic 10,000 meters bronze medalist Lynn Jennings, for example, takes such a supplement three times a week. Others take megavitamins—tablets that

CARBOHYDRATE-RICH FOODS

FOOD	SERVING SIZE	CARBOHYDRATES (G.)
Bagel	1	31
Bread	1 slice	12
Cereal	1 cup	24
English muffin	1	30
Oatmeal	½ cup	12
Pancake	1	18
Pretzels	1 ounce	21
Spaghetti	1 cup	34
Rice	1 cup	50
Waffle	1	17

contain as much as 800 percent of the daily allowances of certain vitamins—to "supercharge" themselves for greater performance. The reasoning behind this approach is that if 100 percent is good, 500 percent must be great.

Do supplements and megavitamins really help? That's a good question. Without a doubt, vitamin supplements can reverse the effects of vitamin deficiencies in runners. At the very least, the belief that vitamins work can have psychological benefits for many runners, especially those who worry about their diets.

But when it comes down to it, supplements and megavitamins have not been shown to directly improve performance significantly in healthy runners.

Can vitamin supplements and/or megavitamins be harmful? Ordinarily, one-size-fits-all supplements appear to be safe. And excess water-soluble vitamins (B complex and C) are simply flushed out in the urine.

But taking large doses of fat-soluble vitamins (A, D and E) can be toxic. Excess vitamins A and D, for example, can damage the nervous system and kidneys. Megadoses of vitamin C can irritate the bowels, causing diarrhea. And some of the B-complex vitamins can also produce toxic reactions that are less noticeable at first but, over time, may cause permanent nerve damage.

TIPS FROM THE TOP

SUPPLEMENTS

Most elite runners interviewed for this book supplement their diets with vitamins and minerals. Here, several top runners explain why.

Steve Brace, 1992 British Olympic marathoner: "I take a multivitamin to make up for any deficiencies I have in my diet. Physiologically, it is vital to be 100 percent to stand up to the rigors of heavy training."

Steve Holman, 1992 U.S. Olympian at 1500 meters: "I take one multivitamin daily to fill in any possible nutritional deficiencies."

Don Janicki, 2:11 marathoner: "I take a multivitamin because training takes a lot out of me. My regular diet doesn't provide everything."

Anne Marie Lauck, member of the 1995 U.S. World Track and Field Championships team at 10,000 meters: "I take two multivitamins, iron, vitamin C, vitamin E and garlic. This way I make sure I'm getting the proper nutrients, and because of that I'm rarely sick."

Lorraine Moller, 1992 Olympic Marathon bronze medalist: "I take mineral supplements because I have a tendency to be low in minerals—iron, calcium, magnesium, selenium, silicon, zinc, potassium and chromium. I also take vitamins C, B-complex and E, as well as ginseng, choline and royal jelly. I do feel better if I take supplements."

Cathy O'Brien, two-time U.S. Olympic marathoner (1988 and 1992): "I take a multivitamin, vitamin C, vitamin E, beta-carotene and iron. I don't know if it helps training, but I want to make sure I'm not depleted."

Sonia O'Sullivan, 1992 Irish Olympian at 3000 meters: "I take a multivitamin with iron. I'm covered each day in case I miss out on any specific vitamin."

Jon Sinclair, two-time U.S. Olympic Marathon Trials qualifier (1988 and 1992): "I take iron, calcium and vitamin E. In my opinion, iron is an absolute necessity for distance runners because of all the heavy pounding their muscles and red blood cells endure."

Steve Spence, 1991 World Marathon Championships bronze medalist and a 1992 Olympic marathoner: "I'm a lacto-ovovegetarian, and to ensure that I don't miss required nutrients in my diet, I take a multivitamin plus iron and a mineral supplement every day."

Mineral Wealth

Minerals are important for growth, water balance, muscular contraction and regulation of cellular metabolism. As with vitamins, mineral supplements will help if a runner has a deficiency. But they don't have an effect if a runner is getting enough minerals. And like vitamins, megadoses can sometimes have deleterious effects.

Calcium. Calcium, the most abundant mineral in the body, is important for muscle contraction, blood clotting, transmission of nerve impulses and the development and maintenance of strong bones. Healthy adults need a minimum of 800 milligrams of calcium daily— depending on their age, women need 1,000 to 1,500 milligrams. But even if calcium intake is adequate, the body may not be absorbing the mineral efficiently, depending on various factors. If intake is low, the body calls upon its calcium reserves in bones to meet the needs, weakening the bones. Since women in general have less bone density than men, they have less calcium stored there; women runners are therefore at greater risk for stress fractures and, in the long term, osteoporosis. Women runners especially should make sure they get enough calcium in their diets.

Dairy foods, legumes and some green vegetables are by far the richest sources of calcium. Like vitamins, minerals are best obtained from food, although supplements may be needed to correct deficiencies.

Electrolytes. During exercise the body loses electrolytes (sodium, potassium, chloride) through sweat. Normally, ordinary foods eaten in ordinary amounts provide adequate amounts of these minerals, but supplements are available for the athlete who believes he needs more.

In the past, much has been made of beer as a source of electrolyte replacement. But when you consider that it's also a diuretic—causing the body to lose fluid—the electrolyte-replacement value of beer gets canceled out. Water and sports drinks are what most elites choose to drink after a race or hard workout.

Iron. Iron is a trace mineral necessary for the formation of hemoglobin, a blood component that delivers oxygen throughout the body. Iron deficiency can lead to anemia, causing fatigue during exertion, sluggishness and loss of appetite—three things a runner doesn't need or want. According to theory, the impact of running may break up red blood cells in the soles of the feet. Iron deficiency—or at least lowered iron levels—may be likely among women runners who menstruate (losing iron in monthly loss of blood). "I include iron with vitamin C in my diet to prevent anemia," says 2:34 marathoner Joy Smith. "Without it, I just wouldn't have the energy I need to train."

Diet also plays a role in iron deficiency. If you're not eating enough meat, fish, poultry, eggs, vegetables and cereals, you could be

FOOD SOURCES OF SELECTED MINERALS

NUTRIENT	DAILY VALUE	FOOD SOURCES
Calcium	1,000 mg.	Milk, cheese, green leafy vegetables, salmon, dried beans
Chromium	*	Meat, whole grains, fortified cereals, broccoli
Iron	18 mg.	Meat, poultry, fish, eggs, beans, nuts, dried fruits, leafy green vegetables, enriched pasta, bread
Magnesium	400 mg.	Green leafy vegetables, whole grains, seafood, bananas, nuts, apricots, beans
Phosphorus	1 g.	Almost all foods: especially fish, meat, poultry, eggs, milk, peas, processed foods
Potassium	3,500 mg.	Most plant foods (especially oranges, bananas, potatoes), yogurt, milk, meat, poultry
Selenium	*	Fish, red meat, grains, eggs
Zinc	15 mg.	Meat, seafood, eggs, milk, beans, whole grains

*No Daily Value. The 1989 Estimated Safe and Adequate Daily Dietary Intake for chromium is 50–200 mcg. The Recommended Dietary Allowance of selenium is 55–70 mcg. for adults.

setting yourself up for iron deficiency problems. Iron supplements are available, but are not always well-absorbed; it's preferable to boost your iron intake through foods rather than pills.

Pre-race Meals: Dinner Is Served

A staple in any marathoner's pre-race ritual is the pasta dinner the night before. Take a look at the runners making one…two…sometimes three trips back to the food line. "Hey," they say, stuffing in another forkful, "I have to run a marathon tomorrow, and this is my last meal."

Most are making two mistakes that elites rarely make: (1) They're overeating, which will make it tough to sleep that night; and (2) more important, they really do think that this is the last meal before the marathon. Overnight the body gets hungry again, and runners who head to the starting line—especially a marathon starting line—without putting something in the tank in the morning have sometimes not eaten for 12 hours.

The problem is that most races start very early in the morning and that doesn't leave much time for breakfast. Pre-race jitters also affect digestion in some runners: What would normally exit the stomach in two hours now takes longer. What to do? Most elite runners eat a light meal, primarily carbohydrates, one to four hours prior to competition.

Elite athletes come up with their ideal pre-race meal by trying out several different meals—bagels, bananas, carbohydrate drinks—in practice, before they settle on one for race day.

Sonia O'Sullivan's pre-race meal, for example, consists of bread or cereal, coffee, perhaps a banana and lots of water. Masters runner Ken Popejoy has found through more than 20 years of racing that it's best for him to race after eating a chicken club sandwich. Anne Marie Lauck prefers to drink coffee as her pre-race meal, as does Todd Williams.

Eat to Recover

The scene in the elite runners' tent immediately following a big road race is one of organized confusion. It's crowded, busy, full of sweat and heat. Some runners have smiles on their faces because they've run well; others are less jubilant. But one thing is constant: All elites are eating or drinking something to replenish energy in their depleted muscles. And they don't waste any time.

If a runner is not careful and skips refueling or doesn't eat right following an intense effort, dead legs and that overall tired feeling can linger for days or weeks. Doughnuts and scrambled eggs won't do the trick—too few carbohydrates. "Immediately after a hard workout or

TIPS FROM THE TOP

WHAT THE ELITES EAT

Steve Brace, 1992 British Olympic marathoner: "I eat a high-carbo-hydrate diet and drink a lot of water, which is a must for any runner. I try for six to eight glasses of water a day."

Lynn Jennings, 1992 Olympic 10,000 meters bronze medalist: "I believe in variety, so I eat several different kinds of foods to cover my nutritional needs. I also make my choices in moderation and don't overeat. And for success in running, as well as good health, I believe in a low-fat diet, so I watch my fat intake."

Janis Klecker, 1992 U.S. Olympic marathoner: "I eat a high-carbo-hydrate, low-fat diet with moderate protein and some red meat to avoid anemia."

Anne Marie Lauck, member of the 1995 U.S. World Track and Field Championships team at 10,000 meters: "I follow a well-balanced diet and eat a lot. I try to stay away from fatty or excessively sugary foods. I don't eat a lot of red meat—because of the higher fat content—but I do eat chicken and fish. And I also eat lots of fruits, grains, pastas and vegetables."

Cathy O'Brien, two-time U.S. Olympic marathoner (1988 and 1992): "I eat lots of fruits and vegetables—from a health standpoint, not so much for performance, although they keep my energy level up. In addition, I watch my fat intake and eat as few processed foods as possible. I also drink lots of water."

Sonia O'Sullivan, 1992 Irish Olympian at 3000 meters: "I think the important thing is to eat a little a lot, rather than a lot a little. In other words, I eat four to six small meals a day rather than three large meals. It keeps my body on an even keel because I'm giving it food when it needs it, not waiting four to five hours between meals and then overeating because of hunger."

PattiSue Plumer, two-time Olympian (1988 at 3000 meters, 1992 at 3000 and 1500 meters): "I don't have a special diet, but I do eat a low-fat, high-carbohydrate diet naturally. I mean that I don't plan it, it just happens."

Ric Sayre, 1983 Los Angeles Marathon winner and elite masters runner: "I've been a vegetarian for 21 years. My diet is very low in fat and very high in carbohydrates. I believe this diet works well for endurance athletes."

PRE-RACE CARBOHYDRATE FOODS

	CARBOHYDRATES (G.)*	CALORIES*
Food		
Raisins (1 cup)	112	440
Bagel (1)	79	200
Banana (1)	61	230
Exceed Sports Bar (1)	54	360
Yogurt (8 oz.)	43	267
Power Bar (1)	40	225
Oatmeal (1 cup)	30	140
Pancakes (3)	24	240
Apple (1)	20	80
Granola bar (1)	17	130
Grapes (1 cup)	16	58
Wheat bread (1 slice)	12	60
Beverages		
High-carbo drink	70–90	280–360
Apple juice (1 cup)	30	120
Orange juice (1 cup)	29	120
Skim milk (1 cup)	12	85

*Values from labels and U.S. Department of Agriculture.

long training run it's important to refuel your body either by drinking a high carbo drink (such as Ultra Fuel) or by eating fruits or other carbos," says 2:34 marathoner Joy Smith.

The first four hours after exercise is a crucial time period that permits greater synthesis of muscle glycogen (that is, the replacement of glycogen lost during exercise with new glycogen gained through eating or drinking). Consuming complex carbohydrates in solid food, such as fruit and breads, or simple carbohydrates in energy-replacement drinks immediately after exercise and then every 15 minutes for the next few hours will enhance muscle glycogen synthesis. Doing this—instead of eating one big meal an hour after a race—maintains

FROM CHIPS AND BEER TO ENERGY BARS AND WATER

Todd Williams, 1992 U.S. Olympian at 10,000 meters, knows firsthand the importance of nutrition for runners. Back when he was a runner at the University of Tennessee, Williams struggled on the track, in part because he had a taste for chips and beer. It wasn't until after Williams cleaned up his diet that he blossomed into one of the top runners in the United States and indeed the world (tenth place in the 10,000 meters at Barcelona).

As Williams puts it, "I'm the kind of guy who has to watch his diet. With my metabolism, even when I'm running 100 miles a week, if I eat three huge meals a day, have a snack at night and then drink some beers on the weekend, I'll gain weight—and that will hurt my running."

A typical day's eating. "I run at 6:30 in the morning and afterward I'll have four pancakes, a bowl of oatmeal, orange juice and a couple glasses of water. It's high-carbohydrate and it gets me going for the day. For lunch I'll eat a Power Bar or two. I'm going to run again in a couple of hours, and Power Bars are pretty much the best thing I can eat; they give me energy and don't upset my stomach. For dinner typical fare would be grilled salmon, rice, a plain baked potato and water or a Diet Coke."

The drink that refreshes. "I rarely drink alcohol. Two or three times a year I'll have a few beers, usually to celebrate the end of a season or a big race. Other runners drink more often, and maybe they can get away with it. Really, I think it's up to the individual. But for me, I know my metabolism can't break it down. And because it will affect my running, beer is something that I don't have to have. I'd rather have a big glass of diet Coke."

Not much fat. "Chips and salsa are history. There are other ways I try to cut fat out of my diet. If I use dressing on my salad, I make sure it's low-fat. I don't put butter on things that usually go with butter, like baked potatoes. I'll have marinara sauce instead of alfredo sauce on pasta. Stuff like that helps keep my body fat low, around 4½ percent, when I'm training heavily."

One cup or two? "I don't drink coffee a whole lot when I'm training. It's a diuretic, and I try to keep as much water in me as possible. I do use coffee, however, the morning of road races, say a 10-K. I'm not good with food in my stomach before a race, and a 10-K is short enough that I feel I don't need to eat something beforehand (a marathon would be another story, but I haven't run one of those yet). So I'll get up a few hours before the race and go for a jog, then come back and have one or two cups of coffee with lots of water to prevent dehydration. The caffeine in those two cups gets me up for the race."

higher blood glucose and insulin concentrations, which in turn makes greater absorption of energy into the muscles possible.

Eating to Train

The average person needs about 2,000 calories a day. Elite runners who are putting in 9 to 20 miles a day need more, sometimes two to three times more, to restore lost energy. And with an increased emphasis on replacing what the body loses—carbohydrates, proteins, fats, vitamins, minerals and fluids—comes the promise of increased energy from several special diets. Let's look at some of these diets and see if they help or hinder.

Modified Carbohydrate Loading

By now just about everyone who ever laced up a pair of running shoes has heard about the importance of carbohydrates for boosting performance. Indeed, the pre-race pasta dinner has become a ritual, designed to top off the energy—glycogen—stores in the muscles in preparation for race day.

It starts with what's known as the depletion phase: Seven days prior to competition—usually a marathon—a runner will cut carbohydrates from his diet. The combination of low carbohydrate intake along with glycogen burning during daily runs depletes glycogen stores in the leg muscles. After three days these muscles are like angry kids, banging their spoons on the table and shouting, "We want carbos! We want carbos!"

Then, for the next three days, the runner gives the muscles what they want, loading up on breads, pastas and other carbohydrate-rich foods. The starving muscles—the theory goes—take in more carbohydrates because they don't want to be depleted again. The result? A runner has more energy to burn on race day.

Yet all runners are different, and that means the time needed to replace glycogen in the muscles is not a constant. Three days of carbo-reloading might bounce Jane's legs back to normal, but Harry's legs may only be half full. Glycogen depletion has also caused light-headedness and even blackouts in some runners, and may hinder the body's ability to use fat—the source your body turns to when it runs out of glycogen—as an energy source.

Most elite runners shun the traditional carbo depletion and reloading altogether or have come up with a modified version that suits them best. Debbi Kilpatrick-Morris, winner of the 1995 U.S. National Marathon Championships, has her own plan. For three days leading up to a marathon, she simply eats more carbohydrates than usual for

EATING LIKE A CHAMP

Debbi Kilpatrick-Morris, winner of the 1995 U.S. National Marathon Championships, credits part of her surprise success to a high-carbohydrate, low-fat diet, which has energized her for harder training.

Breakfast: One or two bowls of cereal (a mixture of Puffed Wheat and Fruit & Fibre) plus orange juice. "Cereal for breakfast might be old-fashioned," says Kilpatrick-Morris, "but it makes a big difference in my energy level. If I don't get it, I tend to drag. There are a lot of carbohydrates in cereal."

Lunch: Energy shake (two cups of no-fat frozen yogurt, one cup of skim milk, a scoop of Slim Fast—for the vitamin content—a scoop of carbohydrate powder and a banana blended until smooth). "When I run in the morning and again in the evening, I like a lunch that's easily digestible," says Kilpatrick-Morris. "Solid foods can be too bulky. That's why I like my energy shake at noon."

Dinner: Pasta (spaghetti, linguine, macaroni, pierogies) in a red (or on occasion white) sauce. Water—or once a week a glass of red wine—to drink. "Pasta is the staple for dinner," says Kilpatrick-Morris. "It's full of energy and low-fat. The key is to vary it throughout the week so you don't get too bored."

breakfast and lunch (dinner remains constant because she doesn't want to upset her sleep pattern because of extra food). This, coupled with a drastic cutback in Kilpatrick-Morris's training—jogging only three or four miles each day or resting completely—packs more energy into the muscles.

Protein Diets: Go Easy

High-protein diets are used primarily by strength-oriented athletes, like football players and weight lifters. Yet some distance runners feel they need extra protein to strengthen and repair muscle tissue damaged during hard training.

Eggs, beef, fish, chicken, protein and amino acid supplements become staples in the diets of these runners—but with a price. Excess protein and amino acids are converted and stored as fat. High-protein diets can also contain high levels of cholesterol, increasing the risk of coronary disease. Increasing the amount of protein in the diet (to greater than 15 percent) means reducing the intake of other nutrients needed by the body, which could lead to imbalances in, say, carbohydrates. The body can absorb no more than 20 grams of protein at a given time, so providing more in any meal is a wasted effort.

Vegetarian Diets: Much to Choose From

Many runners have adopted some type of vegetarian diet as a way to eat less fat and more carbohydrates. Although strict vegetarians abstain from all meats, fish, poultry and other animal products, other vegetarians allow dairy products (lactovegetarian) or both dairy products and eggs (lacto-ovovegetarian). Most recently, the "new vegetarian" diet even allows the occasional meat dish.

For the most part, vegetarian diets are considered healthy and supply sufficient energy for running. But for those who suffer from low iron levels or anemia—like some women runners—meatless diets may not be the way to go.

Olympic Marathon bronze medalist Lorraine Moller takes vitamin and mineral supplements to help "fill in the gaps" left by her vegetarian diet. Most other elite marathoners who eat some sort of vegetarian diet also take supplements, such as vitamin B$_6$ and iron.

CHAPTER

17

Masters Running

40-PLUS AND STILL GOING STRONG

At a 5-K in Charleston, South Carolina, the gun went off and three runners immediately moved to the front. Two were scholarship athletes at a nearby university; the third was Bob Schlau.

"I finished a close third," Schlau recalls, "and in the chute one of the college kids noticed my gray hair and asked me how old I was."

Schlau told him his age. "And the kid said, 'Wow! I knew you had to be older. But I just can't believe it. You ran a heckuva race.' "

We're all going to slow down. It's as inevitable as the tides, the seasons—or gray hair. But *when* you slow down (and how much you slow down) is really up to the individual. "A lot of the slowing-down process you see in runners is more atrophy than aging," says Schlau. "People give up and say, 'Well, I'm too old. I can't do that any more.' "

Schlau is right. And the proof is the phenomenal success of masters runners in the past decade. To cite just a few: Priscilla Welch winning the New York City Marathon at age 42; John Campbell running a 2:11:04 marathon at age 41; Doug Kurtis cranking out sub-2:20 marathons as though they were weekend long runs; and finally, Eamonn Coghlin's sensational 3:58 mile at age 41.

These and other masters runners have stayed competitive into their forties, fifties and even sixties. Along the way they've learned some secrets to staying fit well past 40. But before we go into that, let's look at what happens to a runner's body as it ages.

Growing Up Is Hard to Do

After the Columbus Marathon one year, Nick Rose, who was not quite yet a masters runner, was talking about the way his training had changed with age. "I used to go hard every day," the British Olympian said. "Then I went hard one day and easy the next. Now

137

SPARKS FLYING

Co-author Ken Sparks, who's in his fifties, is still running and racing at a high level. "The key for me is mixing it up," says Sparks. "I compete at all distances—from 800 meters on the track to the marathon." Here's a look at some of Sparks's records.

RECORD	AGE GROUP	EVENT	TIME
World record	45–49	outdoor 1500 m.	4:00:52
World record	50–54	indoor mile	4:32
World record	50–54	indoor 1500 m.	4:17
World record	50–54	indoor 800 m.	2:03
American record	45–49	outdoor mile	4:13
American record	45–49	indoor 1500 m.	4:04
American record	45–49	indoor 800 m.	1:57
American record	49	marathon	2:33:03

it's hard, then two days easy, then hard again."

Longer recovery from hard workouts is one of the first things masters runners have to cope with. Along with Rose, both Ken Popejoy and Ric Sayre agree that recovery from hard sessions (and even from a single repeat within a track workout) takes more time. Another thing that creeps up with age is decreased flexibility.

Why is that? Elite masters athletes, who take extremely good care of their bodies, don't look much different at 44 than they did at 32. Sure, there are a few more crow's-feet around the eyes, and maybe the hair has thinned or turned gray. But what does this have to do with running a fast 10-K?

As Father Time exerts his effect on the aging athlete, most older runners find themselves unable to maintain the training level they enjoyed when they were younger. Is this a physical limitation or just a lack of motivation? The truth is it's probably both. Research shows that the rate of decrease in performance seems to be related to how hard a runner trains and how motivated he is. Highly motivated masters athletes maintain their performance levels longer than their aging colleagues.

Quality race times are usually maintained well into our thirties, as long as hard training continues. As the aches and pains of training become more noticeable, and injuries seem to be more frequent, athletes don't run as hard or as long, and performance can decrease. Also, specific physiological changes at this time—such as reductions in endurance capacity, muscular strength and running speed—and a change in body composition also affect a runner's ability to race fast. Let's look at how these subtle but significant changes translate into how far or fast you can run.

Less Oxygen Cuts Endurance

Endurance levels peak at about 25 years of age, then slowly decline as we grow older. The rate of decrease, however, depends on activity level and heredity.

THE VOICES OF EXPERIENCE

Jacqueline Gareau, 1980 Boston Marathon winner: "In our mid-thirties we should start figuring out how much recovery we need. Normally, we need a little more after age 35 or 38. For instance, two days of recovery after every hard workout instead of one. And maybe we have to come to terms with doing only two hard workouts a week, not three. This is the smarter way to go, and it will help keep us from overtraining."

Larry Olsen, top masters runner: "When I get out-kicked in a race, I don't panic. I don't attribute that to age, because when I was younger, I didn't have a kick anyway. That wasn't my strength. So during races I'll go out a little faster the first half—I won't run even splits. That'll get me some time in the bank, and then I just hang on."

Bob Schlau, top-ranked masters runner in the world in 1988: "You have to keep at it, keep training hard. I like to use the analogy that if you take a calf and lift it every day until it becomes a cow, eventually you will be able (theoretically) to lift a 400-pound animal. That's what training as a master is like. If you keep at it, you don't fall behind and you see results. But if you take time off, you'll find it harder to get back to your previous level: You won't be able to lift the calf again."

Ken Sparks, world-class masters miler: "One of the things you have to keep working on is mental attitude. You have to fight that supposedly rational voice that says, "I'm 50 years old and I don't have to be doing this stuff anymore.""

TIPS FROM THE TOP

MASTERS RUNNING

Jaqueline Gareau, 1980 Boston Marathon winner: "At 41, I've learned to take it easy and enjoy my running. To keep myself from overdoing it, I cross-train. In the winter I do a lot of cross-country skiing. And even when I'm working hard for a race, I prefer to make my second workout of the day a ride instead of a run. The variety makes training more enjoyable, makes me look forward to my runs, and there's also less chance for injury and illness.

In a nutshell, I still train hard, but I realize that rest is an important factor in that training. More rest for me means better workouts on hard days."

Key workouts: "Once or twice a week I cross-country ski for 1½ to 2 hours instead of run. If it's nice and sunny and I don't feel like running, I enjoy it. But I won't replace a quality workout—a track session or a tempo run—with skiing. I'll replace only the easy runs.

"Afternoon workouts are rides instead of runs: 30 to 40 minutes, concentrating on turnover (about 80 to 90 revolutions per minute) to help keep my legs fast."

Larry Olsen, top masters runner: "Since turning 40 I've started doing what I call mini-surges. I'll do them to activate the fast-twitch muscle fibers, which can become inactive if you just jog through most of your workouts. The surges keep me from getting into a rut, a slow rut."

Key workouts: "Every day, except the day after races, I try to incorporate surges in my normal seven- to nine-mile morning run. The surges—a half-dozen for 30 to 40 seconds at five-mile-race pace—come during the middle mile, giving me plenty of time to warm up and cool down. I'll run them fast, but not all-out. I concentrate on form more than pure speed." (Olsen does surges in addition to his two weekly speed sessions: intervals and a tempo run.)

Most of our loss in endurance is related to changes in cardiovascular function. Your maximum heart rate (220 minus your age) and the amount of blood pumped by your heart per beat decrease with age. The end result is that less oxgen is available to the body.

Bob Schlau, top-ranked masters runner in the world in 1988: "As we get older, we tend to lose both range of motion and flexibility, which help us run fast. To combat this, I stretch and do drills.

"I do the drills twice a week, following my track workouts. It builds quickness and the explosive power of the muscles, and helps keep my stride fluid."

Key workouts: "I do three sets of the following four drills. Each drill covers 15 to 20 steps, or about 60 yards of distance. Rest for about 30 seconds before the next drill."

1. Butt kicks: Jog forward and snap your heel toward your butt during each stride.
2. Skip for height: Skip, trying to go as high as you can. Emphasize knee lift and arm pump.
3. Skip for length: Try to go as far as you can. Emphasize leg extension and arm swing.
4. Bounding: Your cadence is between a walk and a jog. Make each stride a giant step, as far as you can reach—like striding across a series of puddles.

Ken Sparks, world-class masters miler: "I train at a high intensity, doing as much quality as possible. I don't, for instance, do long, easy runs; the farthest I go is nine miles, and I do that at 6:00 pace. I'll also do one or two speed workouts a week. And that's the key: cranking out those speed sessions. Because to stay fast, you have to train fast. You can't slip into that routine where you're running all your workouts in that comfort zone."

Key workouts: "I run my interval sessions on a homemade treadmill in the garage. I mix workouts—some days repeat 400s, some days 200s and others in a ladder (200, 400, 600, 800, then down). My favorite workout is one from my college days: 8 × 400. I'll do each in 62 or 63 seconds, a little faster than my one-mile-race pace. But the key is I use a short rest interval. That keeps the workout close to racelike conditions."

This, along with loss of muscle mass that also comes with age, cuts the ability to consume oxygen. How much? About 15 percent per decade for sedentary individuals (a 30-minute 10-K runner at age 20 who has been inactive for 20 years now runs 43 minutes), 9 percent

TYPICAL TRAINING SCHEDULE FOR BARB FILUTZE

To help lessen the cumulative pounding, Barb Filutze, who qualified for the Olympic Marathon Trials as a masters runner, rides a bike once a week and runs on grass once a week. Her legs are not 24 years old anymore. Yet she still trains hard—witness the speed sessions on Wednesday and Friday.

Sunday		18 mi.
Monday	A.M.	5 mi., 7:00 pace
		4 strides at end
	P.M.	6 mi., 7:30 pace
		10 × 1 min., hard pace
Tuesday	A.M.	9 mi., 7:30 pace
		4 × 30 sec., hard
	P.M.	Stationary bike (15 min.)
Wednesday	A.M.	5 mi., easy
		Track workout:
		5 × 200 m., hard, plus ladder:
		600 m., 800 m., 1000 m., 1400 m., 800 m.
	P.M.	3 mi., easy
Thursday		12 mi. on hills, easy
Friday	A.M.	3 mi., easy
	P.M.	6 mi. with 6 × 3 min. hard
Saturday		10 mi. on grass, easy

for the fitness buff and 5 percent for the masters athlete (a 30-minute 10-K runner at 20 who has kept training hard now runs 33 minutes).

Reaching Your Speed Limit

Just like endurance capacity, muscular strength reaches its maximum between the ages of 20 and 30. In fact, most marathoners run their best times in their late twenties. With few exceptions, after the third decade of life muscle strength begins a slow decline.

The main reasons we lose muscular strength are a gradual decrease in muscle mass caused by aging and, often, less rigorous training. This decrease is most profound in our fast-twitch muscle fibers, which determine our leg speed. At 40 we're no longer as fast as we were at 20 because our fast-twitch muscle fibers no longer contract with the same force as they did 20 years ago.

The best way to preserve muscle mass, and ultimately leg speed, is to continue to train with speedwork and add more strength training to your program. The more muscle mass you have, the more *force* will be behind your muscle contractions. With the decline in aerobic capacity and muscle strength, trying to maintain fast times increases the relative intensity of the workout. This explains why older athletes need more recovery between intense workouts. At 45, for example, we can no longer run 60 miles a week, as we did at 25, without getting injured, but maybe we can run 45 to 50.

What You're Made Of

Over time, your body composition undergoes changes that seem to accelerate after age 60, although they start sooner. Studies show that after age 35, the average person loses a half-pound of muscle and gains one pound of fat every year. That's why Joe Couch Potato gradually gains weight, loses muscle and raises his percentage of body fat. Exercise, of course, changes the equation....

For more active people, just because you're getting older doesn't mean you're destined to get fat and flabby. We do have to face the fact that with increased age and loss of muscle mass, the ratio of muscle mass to fat mass is lower. The overall effect is a greater percentage of body fat, even though you may not actually gain weight. And it's muscle, not fat, that speeds you around the track. More fat and less muscle equals more dead weight to carry around.

But don't be alarmed—as a masters runner, you're probably not overfat. Male elite masters runners have 6 to 8 percent body fat compared with 17 to 20 percent for males over 40 who don't exercise; female elites have 15 to 18 percent body fat compared with 26 to 30 percent for females who don't exercise. To get your body fat measured, see a doctor or a sports-fitness professional. Using calipers to measure skinfold fat percentages is a quick way to estimate body fat.

CHAPTER

18

Women Who Run

TRAINING TO WIN

Women weren't considered distance runners until recently. At the 1960 Olympic Games the longest race for women was 800 meters—just a half-mile. And as late as the 1970s, women were chased out of major marathons by overzealous officials who believed that they were protecting the "weaker sex."

Times have changed. Women's distance running has taken major strides forward, most notably with the first Olympic Marathon for women in 1984, won by Joan Benoit Samuelson.

Experts now know that physiologically, women respond to training like men do. They build endurance and strength like men do. They reap the same benefits from a hard ten-miler, track workout or weight workout that men do. If you need further proof, here it is: Women's running times have come down faster than men's have in the past 20 years. And while male runners still have an edge on female runners in the longer distances, the performance gap is narrowing, particularly in the shorter distances. Evidence like this helps put to rest the tired notion that women don't have what it takes to go the distance.

But while biology isn't necessarily destiny, women's distinct physiology does impact on their training. The question isn't whether female distance runners train differently than male runners (they don't), it's how women runners can reinforce their strengths so that they can train to win. Issues of particular concern to female distance runners are nutrition, menstruation (or lack of it) and pregnancy.

Stop Counting Calories

Simply put, female runners need more calories than inactive women. The typical sedentary woman needs approximately 1,800 calories per day; a female distance runner may need 2,400 to 3,000

CHANGES IN WORLD-RECORD PERFORMANCE TIMES, 1975–1994

World Records	1975	1994	Change (sec.)
Women			
1500 m.	4:01.38	3:50.46	-10.92
Mile	4:29.50	4:15.61	-13.89
3000 m.	8:52.80	8:06.11	-46.69
5000 m.	15:53.60	14:37.78	-75.82
10,000 m.	35:30.50	29:31.78	-358.72
Marathon	2:43:55.00	2:21:06.00	-1369.00
Men			
1500 m.	3:32.16	3:28.86	-3.30
Mile	3:51.10	3:44.39	-6.71
3000 m.	7:35.10	7:25.11	-9.99
5000 m.	13:13.00	12:56.96	-16.04
10,000 m.	27:30.80	26:52.23	-38.57
Marathon	2:08:34.00	2:06:50.00	-104.00

calories per day, depending on her mileage. (A good rule of thumb is about 100 calories per mile.)

"You have to realize that you're eating for performance and not just because it's dinner time," says 2:34 marathoner Joy Smith. "What you're eating is fueling your next workout."

Eating a variety of foods can help ensure that women runners get adequate amounts of vitamins and minerals. The ideal is to take in about 30 percent of calories from fats, 58 percent from carbohydrates and 12 percent from protein.

Also, women runners need to consume adequate amounts of calcium and iron. Calcium is an A-1 priority nutrient for bones. Found in low-fat dairy products, like reduced-fat cheese and skim milk, green leafy vegetables and legumes, calcium helps maintain bone density and fend off stress fractures. Eating a calcium-rich diet also helps thwart the bone-thinning disease osteoporosis, which many women develop in their later years. The Daily Value (DV) for calcium is 1,000 milligrams.

Many women runners take calcium supplements. Others, like Smith, get their calcium from food. "I drink two glasses of skim milk a day, one at breakfast and one at dinner," says Smith.

Iron, found in red meat, shellfish, fish and some fruits and vegetables, allows red blood cells to deliver oxygen from the lungs to the rest of the body. Iron also helps the body release energy. The Daily Value for iron is 18 milligrams. Because women lose iron-rich blood through menstruation, they need to make sure they're getting enough of this essential mineral. "Women need to watch their iron stores," says Laurie Gomez-Henes, member of the 1995 U.S. World Track and Field Championships team at 10,000 meters.

Many women runners take iron supplements; others eat red meat or poultry. "I eat red meat three times a month," says Debbi Kilpatrick-Morris, winner of the 1995 U.S. National Marathon Championships. "I think extra iron helps keep me running strong." Smith concurs. "If a female runner's performance begins to suffer—say, all of a sudden she runs a couple of bad races or is fatigued for a week—I'd look into whether she's getting enough iron."

CAN YOU OUTRUN YOUR PERIOD? MAYBE, MAYBE NOT

World-record performances during menstruation have been known to occur. Then again, some women runners can't get out the door during that time. Here's what the elite runners say.

Debbi Kilpatrick-Morris, winner of the 1995 U.S. National Marathon Championships: "If I'm uncomfortable before race time, I'll take three ibuprofen tablets about an hour beforehand. During training it's another story. Often I'll be running and the cramps will hit—I have to stop running and lie down right there. Usually, after five minutes I'm fine. But if I've gotten up too soon, the cramps will hit again, and I'll have to lie back down for the full five minutes."

Joy Smith, 2:34 marathoner: "Each woman is different. Some women can race through their periods, others can't. If you don't race or train well during those three or four days, you might want to reduce your training. I'll run during that time but only easy runs—nothing hard that will stress my body. If a major race falls on that day, it's just bad luck—I take ibuprofen and do the best I can."

TIPS FROM THE TOP

SEE HOW THEY RUN

Barb Filutze, two-time U.S. Olympic Marathon Trials qualifier (1984 and 1988) and elite masters runner: "I believe women are capable of more training than they think. But they need to eat enough."

Laurie Gomez-Henes, member of the 1995 U.S. World Track and Field Championships team at 10,000 meters: "Women runners are just as competitive as men, work as hard as men and want it just as much as men. But women need to watch their iron stores and be aware of eating disorders."

Jill Hunter, two-time British Olympian (3000 meters in 1988 and 10,000 meters in 1992): "Women runners who don't menstruate regularly should consult a doctor just to be safe, and get enough iron and calcium."

Cathy O'Brien, two-time U.S. Olympic marathoner (1988 and 1992): "Rest is important to avoid injury. Also, you need to balance a healthy attitude—proper nutrition, rest, a good quality of life—with hard training."

PattiSue Plumer, two-time Olympian (1988 at 3000 meters, 1992 at 3000 and 1500 meters): "Too many coaches, particularly male coaches, don't understand the seriousness and pervasiveness of eating disorders. Women runners must eat a healthy diet and, if they are amenorrheic, consult with their doctors."

Lisa Weidenbach, 1985 Boston Marathon champion: "Too much is made of women's weight; women need to eat and train as the men do. It's okay to train vigorously as long as you eat adequately and maintain enough body fat to menstruate."

When Periods Disappear

Many female distance runners develop irregular menstrual periods or stop menstruating altogether, a condition called amenorrhea. Experts don't know what causes amenorrhea, but intense, high-mileage training seems to contribute to this condition, which appears in one out of three female distance runners.

"When my body's under a greater amount of stress—when I'm racing often or doing higher mileage—my menstrual cycle is less frequent," says Annette Peters, 1992 U.S. Olympian at 3000 meters.

TYPICAL TRAINING SCHEDULE FOR LYNN JENNINGS

"My longevity, injury-free career and success speak volumes," says Lynn Jennings, the 1992 Olympic 10,0000 meters bronze medalist. "I take good care of my body and don't overrace or overtrain."

Sunday	14–16 mi., 6:10–6:15 pace
Monday	2 runs (total: 8–10 mi.)
Tuesday	2 runs (total: 10–12 mi.)
Wednesday	Track workout:
	400 m., 0:68
	1600 m., 4:55
	400 m., 0:68
	1600 m., 4:53
	400 m., 0:68
	1600 m., 4:50
	400 m., 0:66
Thursday	2 runs (total: 12–14 mi.)
Friday	4–6 mi., easy pace
Saturday	Race

Excessive weight loss, which reduces body fat, has been linked to amenorrhea as well. A connection between abnormal eating patterns and menstrual dysfunction is well-documented, and eating disorders are prevalent in female runners.

"It's that voice that says, 'Oh, I would be faster if only I was just a little lighter,'" says Smith. "So you lose that pound or two, but that voice is still there.

"What you have to realize is that thinner is not necessarily better. Excessive weight loss can weaken you, lead to amenorrhea and leave you more susceptible to stress fractures. My weight fluctuates from 108 to 114 pounds. I've learned that just because I'm up a few pounds doesn't mean I'm going to run slower times."

In most cases amenorrhea is temporary: Once training and competition stop, normal menstruation occurs and fertility returns. (Although amenorrhea does not always indicate infertility.) Amenorrhea is not always easily reversed, however, and so far no one knows much about the long-term effects of this phenomenon. If you are concerned, consult your doctor.

Does Pregnancy Affect Performance?

When a woman runner gets pregnant, two questions she's apt to ask her doctor are: "Is it safe to run?" and "Will pregnancy affect my performance?"

The answer to both questions is: It depends.

Some female runners have been known to compete during the first three or four months of their pregnancy with no problem. Less than eight months after giving birth to her daughter Katrina, Gwyn Coogan, a 1992 U.S. Olympian at 10,000 meters, ran her best 10,000 meters ever—32:08.

"Some women put in a lot of hard training when they are pregnant," says Coogan. "Not me. I ran for the first three months before I knew I was pregnant, but after that my training tapered off dramatically. I went from 70 miles one week to 60 the next, and so on. I didn't feel comfortable running."

But Coogan says she continued to work out. "I went to the pool every day and swam for a half-hour to an hour. I didn't feel pregnant when I was swimming; the weightlessness felt very good."

Regaining her stride after Katrina was born was more difficult, says Coogan. "It was like starting all over again, but I wasn't discouraged. I went running two weeks after the baby was born. At first I walked for 20 minutes, ran for a mile, walked another 20 minutes and that was it. I gradually progressed to two miles of running, then three miles of running and no walking. At the end of six weeks, I was running five miles at a time, and I finally felt like a runner again. But it took me a full six months to get back into racing shape."

The biggest hurdle Coogan had to face was not improving her time but "not feeling guilty about making time for yourself to run. If running is important to you, it shouldn't be fifteenth on your list," she says.

Research indicates that depending on the circumstances, exercise is not only safe for moms-to-be, it's beneficial. Female athletes seem to have fewer complications with pregnancy and childbirth than nonathletic women.

Before deciding to continue training (including weight training) or running competitively, however, consult your doctor.

Peaking

PLANNING FOR TOP PERFORMANCE

The summer of 1994 was a breakthrough year for Bob Kennedy. Coming into the European track season, the 23-year-old Indiana University graduate had a personal best of 13:14.9 for 5000 meters—a good time, to be sure, but a time that often left Kennedy staring at more backs than a chiropractor at the end of major international races. To run competitively in Europe, Kennedy knew he had to drop his personal record (PR) a good ten seconds.

By the end of the summer Kennedy had done just that, running 13:02.9, the second-fastest time ever by an American and one of the fastest 5000s of all time. "I'm now one of the best 5000-meter runners in the world," says Kennedy.

Kennedy's breakthrough in the summer of 1994 might be chalked up to the inevitable maturation of a gifted runner, which is partly true. But more important, it was because of a plan that Kennedy and his coach Sam Bell had hatched back in January of that year.

In the summer of 1994, Bob Kennedy reached a peak.

When It All Comes Together

Just what is a peak? In a way, peaking is an art form that involves a steady heightening of fitness at the same time that the body is getting needed rest and the mind is sharpening. In short, it's a coming together both mentally and physically for a race or a series of races—because only that race or those races matter. The classic example of someone who knew how to peak is Lasse Viren, who won the 5000 and 10,000 meters at the 1972 and 1976 Olympics and never seemed to run quite as well in between those years.

But before a runner can peak, he has to have a goal. In other words, you have to know what you want to achieve, and then decide how you're going to do it. You have to have a plan.

Mapping Out the Plan

Snow was falling outside the track office at Indiana University in Bloomington as Kennedy and Bell sat down in early January to map out a plan for the year. The European track season was still seven months away, yet Kennedy and Bell knew implicitly what Kennedy wanted to accomplish months down the line.

"We write our workout schedules in three-week blocks," says Kennedy, "and though we knew what the immediate goal was, what I was trying to accomplish in the next three weeks, in the back of my mind, and in Coach Bell's mind, too, was the ultimate goal: what I wanted to do months and months away."

What Kennedy and Bell did was divide the European track season into halves. The first involved a couple of races (two 5000s and a 3000) in July. Kennedy's goal for that time period was to run 13:10 to 13:11 for 5000. The second half kicked off in mid-August with a meet in Zurich. Kennedy's goal for that time period was to run a 13:07 to 13:08.

Obviously, Kennedy's goals had to be rewritten after he ran 13:05 in his first 5000 in Europe. But the point is, Kennedy knew—way back in January—what times he wanted to peak at during the summer. And as the training went along, Kennedy and Bell knew how to tailor his speed workouts to reach those time goals. "We looked at 13:07 to 13:08 as a goal," Kennedy says. "That was a 63-seconds-per-400 pace, so everything on the track was geared around that."

Take Three Steps to the Top

Peaking is not something an elite runner does overnight. It takes months—or even years—to peak. Most elites, like Kennedy, follow a three-step formula to put them at the top of their game.

Step 1: Build a strong base. "Key factors in peaking for a race happen six to nine months before a race," says Kennedy. And he's not just whistling Dixie.

Without a good solid base of distance and strength work in the winter, Kennedy would not have achieved his times in the summer. Throughout January, February and April Kennedy logged 90 to 95 miles a week—long runs, hill workouts and strides in and around his home in Bloomington. In March Kennedy was diagnosed with a stress fracture, and he spent the month riding a stationary bicycle two hours a day to maintain his base.

"At this time of year the most important thing is getting that base-strength work in on a consistent basis," says Kennedy. "That's because you have to build a foundation—that's where the times later in

TAPERING: THE FINAL DAYS

Here is Bob Kennedy's taper for a key race that occurs on a Saturday.

Sunday		Jog 8 mi.
Monday	A.M.	Jog 4 mi.
	P.M.	A hard session at the track: repeat 400s, 600s or 800s
Tuesday	A.M.	Jog 3 mi.
	P.M.	Jog 5 mi.
Wednesday	A.M.	Jog 4 mi.
	P.M.	Back on the track for 200s or 300s at race tempo. "But nothing that will bury me," he says. "I'll be recovered the very next day."
Thursday	A.M.	Jog 3 mi.
	P.M.	Jog 5 mi.
Friday		Easy jogging (7:00 pace): 20 minutes in the morning and 20 minutes at night. "The day before a race I'll run twice a day because it's a habit. But I also do it because jogging helps flush out all the junk in my muscles."
Saturday		Key race

the year really come from. Too many runners rush this phase, or skip it and try to get race-ready in a few weeks. And what you do a few weeks before a meet really has no bearing on how well you race, because you can't get in shape that quickly. In fact, it's detrimental. If you try to get in shape that quickly, you're going to be fatigued. You need to be rested and ready to go if you're going to race well."

In addition, this base-strength phase is important for elites who want to hold their peak over a period of weeks for a series of important races, like the European track season or the fall road races.

Step 2: Run fewer miles, faster repeats. In May and June Kennedy cut his mileage to about 70 miles a week and added intense speedwork to his schedule, running repeat 400s, 600s and 800s two or three times a week. Then, when he felt more fit, he added shorter races to test his fitness. Kennedy won the Prefontaine Classic Mile in

3:54 in early June, then placed fifth in the 1500 meters at the U.S.A. Track and Field Championships a few weeks later. "The reason I ran the 1500 instead of the 5000 at the nationals was that it was very hot down there in Tennessee and, to be honest with you, there was no reason to run a 5000 in the heat," says Kennedy. "You can run only so many 5000s in a season, and I didn't want to waste one."

By the end of June the intensity of his speed sessions was very high. On June 30 Kennedy ran 2 × 600 in 1:30, 4 × 800 in 2:02 and 2 × 400 in 0:57 (all much faster than his 0:63-lap goal pace for the

TIPS FROM THE TOP

PEAKING

It goes without saying that these elite athletes couldn't have set the records they now hold without learning to hold their peaks. Let's see what tips they offer for this key phase.

Steve Brace, 1992 British Olympic marathoner: "Before a key race that I'm peaking for, I get in plenty of rest and stretching, but I also like having hot baths and massage treatments to get my legs really loose and ready."

Barb Filutze, two-time U.S. Olympic Marathon Trials qualifier (1984 and 1988) and elite masters runner: "If I can, I like to simulate the course I'll be racing on. If there's a hill at three miles, for example, I run a route at home that has a hill at three miles."

Steve Holman, 1992 U.S. Olympian at 1500 meters: "To peak you have to be not only physically ready but mentally ready as well. By that I mean you have to have confidence in your training. If you enter a race with doubts about your training, you've already lost. Whether or not your training has been good, at that point, is another matter."

Don Janicki, 2:11 marathoner: "How I peak is simple. I won't enter a major race, like a marathon, unless I know I'm ready for it. All my training has to click. I have to be healthy and ready to race before I step to the starting line."

Lorraine Moller, 1992 Olympic Marathon bronze medalist: "Focus. Focus. Focus. I get honed in to the race by making a conscious effort to tune out all that is not pertinent to my good performance. I ask people around me to help and support me in this."

5000). At this time, rest within a workout also came into play. Earlier in the year, for example, Kennedy might have been resting only a minute between, say, repeat 400s. Now, with the emphasis on speed more than endurance, he would get a fuller rest—say, jog another 400 meters—before beginning the next repeat.

Kennedy's mileage dropped further in July—down to about 60 miles per week, tapered. Then he ran 13:05 and 13:02 in Europe. He returned home to Indiana for a few weeks of training, and by mid-August, with his goal races just around the corner, Kennedy had further cut his mileage to about 50 miles a week. He flew back to Europe fresh, not overraced and tired. He still had some good racing left in his legs.

August 17 was Kennedy's goal race of the year. He and Bell had made that a red letter date since January. Originally, that meet—in Zurich—was to be the day Kennedy ran 13:07. But since he'd already run 13:02 a few weeks before, Kennedy's goals had to be reevaluated—to running sub-13:00 and winning races outright in Europe.

Step 3: Taper. The third and final piece of the peaking puzzle is the taper, a noticeable cut in training in the final days before a key race. In Kennedy's case—he was running a 5000—the taper lasted about a week. For a marathon it may be two weeks.

As the taper begins and a runner logs fewer miles each day and each week, tired muscles get needed rest and the carbohydrate stores in the muscles refuel to levels higher than at any other time during training. The result is a high energy level during all runs and a crispness in the legs during speedwork.

This physical well-being translates into a psychological one as well. Gone is the mental fatigue that accompanies hard training. The mind is now rested, alert and ready to go. With a good taper, the elite runner is not only ready to run fast, he believes that he will run fast, too.

So at this time Kennedy was also coming to his mental peak as well. "All year long when I'm out running, I think about who I'll be racing against and I mentally put myself in a race situation," he says. "By the time I get to a key race, that is all very clear in my mind."

When he steps to the line, Kennedy knows what he wants to accomplish. His body is rested, his mind is set, he's ready to go. All he has to do is—ahem—just do it.

Unfortunately, there are other factors besides basework, speed sessions, sharpening and tapering that come into play when elites want to peak for a race. A major variable is weather. On August 17 in Zurich it rained cats and dogs during the 5000 and the wind kicked up. Kennedy ran a competitive race (13:12), but it was slower than he'd hoped. "Zurich was rough," he says. "The weather was crap. I felt horrible because I made the mistake of trying to race a major 5000 coming off a plane. But the bright side is that a 13:12 is now a horrible race for me. Last year it would have been my best ever."

Kennedy returned home from Europe the brightest U.S. track star in many seasons—and it was because of, in part, a well-thought-out peak.

How Long Can You Stay at the Summit?

A common sight on the elite road-race circuit: A runner has a string of races in which she runs better than ever. This string may last for a few weeks or a couple of months—then the roof caves in, and she's struggling to run times that she used to cruise through in practice. What happened?

"She rode her peak too long," says Steve Spence, the 1991 World Marathon Championships bronze medalist and a 1992 Olympic marathoner. A peak, once an elite athlete has achieved it, is a double-edged sword. You feel great. Your fitness level has never been higher; you're fresh and ready to go. Each race is better than the last. So why not go for another win or PR?

But on the other side, time is running out. Each race is chipping away at your aerobic fitness foundation, the basework you did months beforehand. Smart runners know to stop racing before the foundation is totally gone—leading not only to poorer race times but sometimes to illness and injury. "You have to learn when to quit while you're ahead," says Spence.

Generally speaking, most athletes who have put in a couple of good months of base-building and strength work before the racing season can hold a peak for 8 to 12 weeks. And only if they're racing the middle distances, 5-Ks to 10-Ks, and not doing a hard 10-K every week. "You can't be doing 10-Ks all the time," says elite road racer Keith Dowling. "They take too much out of you."

So the verdict is in: Four to eight hard races and it's time to take it easy for a while and recharge the batteries.

Bob Schlau on Peaking for a Marathon

At 37 Bob Schlau was the oldest qualifier for the 1984 U.S. Olympic Marathon Trials. (You have to break 2:20 to qualify.) Four years later, in 1988, Schlau again was the oldest runner to qualify. Bob Schlau obviously knows a thing or two about peaking for a marathon.

TYPICAL TRAINING SCHEDULE FOR BOB KENNEDY

This week is typical during Bob Kennedy's early speed-work phase of his peaking plan. At this point, Kennedy, a 1992 U.S. Olympian at 5000 meters, has put in a good two to three months of base training and his key race is still months away. Note that the mileage is still high and the speedwork fast—but not as fast as later—with not much rest between each repeat. His race on Saturday is a good effort, but Kennedy hasn't peaked for it.

Sunday		12 mi., gentle (6:00–6:30 pace)
Monday	A.M.	5 mi., gentle
	P.M.	Road run 15-K; mile splits—5:05, 5:15, 4:59, 5:12, 4:19, 5:08, 5:25, 4:51, 5:10; total time—47:12
		1 mi. cooldown
Tuesday	A.M.	6 mi., gentle
	P.M.	5 mi., gentle
Wednesday	A.M.	4 mi., gentle
	P.M.	Track workout:
		3 mi. warm-up
		5 × 800 m. 2:08, 2:07, 2:06, 2:02, 2:04; 1:40 rest between each
		2 mi. cooldown
Thursday	A.M.	5 mi., gentle
	P.M.	7 mi., gentle
Friday	A.M.	4 mi., gentle
	P.M.	4 mi., gentle
Saturday	A.M.	2 mi., gentle
	P.M.	3000 m. race, 7:44.93
		4 mi. cooldown

"A key to peaking for a marathon is my last 20-miler. I do it four weeks before the race. I used to do it two weeks before, but I think that's a mistake. We often underestimate the cumulative nature of the training that we do, how long those 20-milers will stay with you. Plus, the base that you build stays with you longer than you might think.

"After my last 20-miler I have plenty of time to rest up and continue my sharpening, my speed sessions. Basically, I run the same types of speed sessions to peak for a marathon as I do for a 10-K, but they're not as fast. There's no need, if I'm going to be averaging 5:30 miles in a marathon, to go out and run 4:45 miles in practice. I'm never going to use that speed.

"A sharpening session on the track for a marathon in which I want to run a 5:30 pace would be four to six miles at a 5:00 pace—about 30 seconds faster per mile than marathon pace. Or I might do a three-mile time trial in 15:30, something that's faster than marathon pace but not too fast. I've often done a three-mile time trial two weeks before a marathon. It's a good way to do some running a little faster than race pace; if you do it evenly, it doesn't waste you.

"My taper begins about ten days before the marathon with a day off. Seven days before, I might run 12 miles, which is my last semi-long run. Then I drop it down to 6 to 8 miles a day for two days and 5 miles a day for two days. Two days before the race I take a day off. That's because I like to run a little the day before a marathon to keep me loose. My taper gets me rested, but I'm also still running. I find if I take too many days off right before a race, I get stale. I think it's best to work some days off in and around your running days to still be in a training rhythm.

"The final thing I do in my taper is stretch more. When I start cutting back the miles and the speed sessions, I tend to lose a little bit of range of motion in my legs. Stretching works to counteract that without the pounding of speedwork."

Lynn Jennings: "I Was Supremely Ready"

Not every elite runner builds for one key race or series of races. There are nontraditional types of peaks as well. Lynn Jennings, the 1992 Olympic 10,000 meters bronze medalist, explains how she peaked several times in 1992.

"I don't use the word peaking—and neither does my coach, John Babington—but in 1992 I was supremely ready for the World Cross-Country Championships (first overall), the Olympic 10,000-meter Trials (first), the Olympics (bronze medal) and the U.S. Cross-Country Championships (first). That was March, June, August and November all in one year.

"I ran well at all four of those races through a combination of three things: judicious amounts of speedwork, appropriate amounts of rest and a large foundation of endurance training.

"When I got close to a key race, I would decrease my miles and do faster work. Four weeks before the Olympics I ran 70 miles, then 50, then 40, then 30. During those last few weeks I was doing very high quality track sessions. I would run 3 miles of speedwork several different ways. A workout could include 200s, miles and 1½-mile runs—all much faster than 10-K race pace. The last great track workout I did before the Olympic final included a mile in 4:42, an 800 in 2:14 and several 400s in 0:61, with lots of rest in between.

"After each key race I would run easy for a week or two, then start training for the next race. I didn't take any time off from training. In fact, I haven't taken a day off intentionally in the past seven years.

"That year, 1992, was a bit of an anomaly for me. I pretty much trained and raced the whole year. But I stayed healthy and ran well. It worked."

CHAPTER

20

Short-Distance Races: 5-Ks and 10-Ks

RUNNING FAST

The Carlsbad 5000 in Carlsbad, California, is one of the premier 5-K road races in the world. On race day there's not just one race but a series of races beginning with the citizen's race and ending with the elite women's and elite men's races. Recreational runners crowd the course and watch elite women break the tape in 15 minutes and elite men cross the line in 13 minutes. Then these runners shake their heads, wondering, "How the heck do those people get to be that *fast*?"

Genetics plays a big role in separating recreational runners from the elites. But other than that, the major difference is that elite runners run fast several days a week in practice. They race fast because they train fast. Yet training fast does not simply mean going out to the track and running till you drop. Elites won't train fast until they've done preparatory work—and more goes into a track workout than you might think.

First, Run Long

Before these top athletes work on their speed, they establish an adequate aerobic foundation. In other words, their bodies have to be strong enough to withstand the more intense speed workouts. Elites—even those concentrating on races as short as 5-K—spend the initial part of their training season building a base (discussed in chapter 3) of about 70 to 90 miles per week. To do this, they'll increase their mileage each week by about 10 percent. Beyond this level, studies show, more mileage yields little additional aerobic capacity. In

PACING YOURSELF

Choosing the right pace to start is important. Here is a simple formula that can be used for interval workouts.

1. Calculate the average mile pace for the race distance. For example, a 15:32 5-K would average out to 5:00 miles.
2. Then calculate the average time for the 400, 800 and 1200 meters. For example, 75 seconds for the 400, 2:30 for the 800 and 3:45 for the 1200.

SUGGESTED PACE CHART FOR INTERVAL WORKOUTS

RACE PACE AVERAGE MILE	400 M.	800 M.	1200 M.	MILE
4:30	0:60–0:66	2:07–2:13	3:15–3:20	4:22–4:28
4:40	0:62–0:68	2:12–2:18	3:22–2:28	4:32–4:38
4:50	0:64–0:70	2:17–2:23	3:29–3:35	4:42–4:48
5:00	0:67–0:73	2:22–2:28	3:37–3:43	4:52–4:58
5:10	0:69–0:75	2:27–2:33	3:44–3:50	5:02–5:08
5:20	0:72–0:78	2:32–2:38	3:52–3:58	5:12–5:18
5:30	0:74–0:80	2:37–2:43	4:00–4:05	5:22–5:28
5:40	0:77–0:83	2:42–2:48	4:07–4:13	5:32–5:38
5:50	0:79–0:85	2:47–2:53	4:14–4:20	5:42–5:48
6:00	0:82–0:88	2:52–2:58	4:22–4:28	5:52–5:58
6:10	0:84–0:90	2:57–3:03	4:29–4:35	6:02–6:08

other words, if you're training for shorter distance races, running 100 miles a week won't help you any more than running 75 miles a week.

Base building is done over a period of months. Steve Spence, the 1991 World Marathon Championships bronze medalist and a 1992 Olympic marathoner, recommends eight to ten weeks of uninterrupted training to build a solid base. During that time Spence runs easy, getting used to the increased mileage. Toward the end of the period, he adds transitional workouts, such as tempo runs or hill repeats, preparing him for the faster work ahead. Spence resists the temptation to race during this phase.

3. Subtract two to eight seconds from these times to find your time zone for interval workouts. For example, 67 to 73 seconds for 400s, 2:22 to 2:28 for 800s and 3:37 to 3:43 for 1200s.

This formula can be used to plan interval workouts for short-distance races—anything between 5-K and 10-K. (See the pace chart below.)

RACE PACE AVERAGE MILE	400 M.	800 M.	1200 M.	MILE
6:20	0:87–0:93	3:02–3:08	4:37–4:43	6:12–6:18
6:30	0:89–0:95	3:07–3:13	4:44–4:50	6:22–6:28
6:40	0:92–0:98	3:12–3:18	4:52–4:58	6:32–6:38
6:50	0:94–1:40	3:17–3:23	5:00–5:05	6:42–6:48
7:00	1:37–1:43	3:22–3:28	5:07–5:13	6:52–6:58
7:10	1:39–1:45	3:27–3:33	5:17–5:20	7:02–7:08
7:20	1:42–1:48	3:32–3:38	5:22–5:28	7:12–7:18
7:30	1:44–1:50	3:37–3:43	5:29–5:35	7:22–7:28
7:40	1:47–1:53	3:42–3:48	5:37–5:43	7:32–7:38
7:50	1:49–1:55	3:47–3:53	5:44–5:50	7:42–7:48
8:00	1:52–1:58	3:52–3:58	5:52–5:58	7:52–7:58

Then, Run Fast

"To race fast one must train fast," says Lynn Jennings, the 1992 Olympic 10,000 meters bronze medalist. "Don't be afraid to work hard on the track." Speedwork can be done anywhere—on the track, on roads, on park trails, on golf course fairways and even on treadmills. Of the various workouts (see chapter 4), the one most elites use to get in shape for 5-Ks, 8-Ks or 10-Ks is interval training, which balances hard efforts (repeats) with rest or recovery intervals.

Interval training is done at about 80 to 90 percent of a runner's aerobic capacity. A runner gives his body small doses—30 seconds

TIPS FROM THE TOP

RUNNING FAST

All elite runners include speedwork in their training regimens. Listen to these voices of experience.

Steve Brace, 1992 British Olympic marathoner: "When doing speedwork, distance runners should aim to keep recovery periods short."

Budd Coates, three-time U.S. Olympic Marathon Trials qualifier (1984, 1988 and 1992): "Concentrate on good form and make sure your speed pace is relative to your present fitness level."

Laurie Gomez-Henes, member of the 1995 U.S. World Track and Field Championships team at 10,000 meters: "After your base training period, do two or three sessions of interval training a week."

Don Janicki, 2:11 marathoner: "Work with people who are trying to reach the same goal; in other words, someone who is running the same distance and is at your level."

Anne Marie Lauck, member of the 1995 U.S. World Track and Field Championships team at 10,000 meters: "Make sure you and your coach are well-versed in speed training, as improper techniques and workouts lead to injuries more than other types of training. Start gradually and have a plan."

Lorraine Moller, 1992 Olympic Marathon bronze medalist: "The more intense the faster sessions, the more recovery you need. I always hold back a little and find I get better returns. I save the 100 percent eyeball-out effort for races."

Cathy O'Brien, two-time U.S. Olympic marathoner (1988 and 1992): "I

to, say, four minutes—of running at this intense level, and over time the body adapts to that level of running and the stresses that go with it (lactic acid in muscles and harder breathing). During this phase of your training you may have to reduce your overall mileage to allow for greater recovery from these workouts.

Among its many benefits, interval training (1) increases both aerobic and anaerobic capacity, (2) aids muscle fiber recruitment and improves your speed and (3) enables a runner to reach maximal aerobic capacity quickly. On the downside, because of its intensity, interval prefer to do most of my speedwork on the roads, including short-duration pickups (one to two minutes) and longer intervals (one- to two-mile repeats), as well as tempo runs of four to seven miles."

Ken Popejoy, world masters champ at 1500 meters in 1991 and 1993: "For a masters runner, speed training is probably the biggest need. We find that our speed is falling off fast and we need to work harder to bring out what is left of our speed."

Reuben Reina, 1992 U.S. Olympian at 5000 meters: "Don't rush into speed training. Prepare your body for the stress you will be putting on it. Gradually start to integrate your intervals with slower, controlled workouts."

Nick Rose, two-time British Olympian at 10,000 meters (1980 and 1984) and elite masters runner: "Don't do too much when you are as old as I am. The more speed-oriented the session, the greater the chance of injuries."

Steve Spence, 1991 World Marathon Championships bronze medalist and a 1992 Olympic marathoner: "After a solid base is built, start introduction of speed gradually with transitional workouts such as road fartlek and hills."

Lisa Weidenbach, 1985 Boston Marathon champ: "Short recovery is very important for speed training. I do 5 × 1 mile repeats with 90 seconds rest rather than two to three ml\inutes. You do sacrifice around five seconds per mile, but I don't care. It makes me strong."

training and high mileage do not mix. Interval training also raises the risk of injury. Finally, it's psychologically taxing—you need to be motivated to step on the track.

Running Intervals

When planning interval speedwork, a runner decides the types of repeat workouts and intervals based on his racing goals and current level of fitness.

Quality control: Set the pace. Most elites run interval workouts in

QUANTITY CHART: DETERMINING NUMBER OF REPEATS

	SHORT INTERVALS				LONG INTERVALS			
	400 m.		800 m.		1200 m.		Mile	
WEEKLY MILEAGE	EFFORT/REST RATIO							
	1:1	1:2	1:1	1:2	1:½	1:1	1:½	1:1
20–30	6	8	3	5	2	3	2	3
31–35	6*	8*	3*	5*	2*	3*	2*	3*
36–40	8	10	4	6	3	4	3	4
41–45	8*	10*	4*	6*	3*	4*	3*	4*
46–50	10	12	5	7	4	5	4	5
51–55	10*	12*	5*	7*	4*	5*	4*	5*
56–60	12	14	6	8	5	6	4	5
61–65	12*	14*	6*	8*	5*	6*	4*	5*
66–70	14	16	7	9	6	7	5	6
71–75	14*	16*	7*	9*	6*	7*	5*	6*
76–80	16	18	8	10	7	8	6	7

*Increased effort

which the effort is less in distance than the actual race but the pace is slightly faster than race pace. In other words, low distance but high quality. "Begin gradually, both in intensity and volume," says 2:34 marathoner Joy Smith. "Learn to develop a sense of pace. As you become stronger, reduce the recovery time while maintaining the intensity."

Quantity: How many repeats? After figuring the pace for the workout, the next step is deciding the number of repeats to run. Factors to consider include weekly mileage, how fast you're going to run the repeats (two seconds faster than race pace or eight seconds faster) and the distance of each repeat.

As your mileage goes up, so does the number of intense efforts you can do. Also, as the intensity of the efforts goes up, the number of repeats drops. Keep in mind that as you go from short intervals (200 to 800 meters) to long intervals (1000 meters and up), you should decrease the number of repeated efforts.

Interval: How long to rest? Finally, determine how long you need to rest (the interval) between repeats. As the intensity goes up, the rest period inevitably becomes longer. But the goal is to keep the rest period as short as possible and still maintain the pace.

In balancing the effort and the rest periods, a ratio such as 1:1 or 1:2 is set up. This ratio simply means that the rest period is either the same (1:1) or twice as long (1:2) as the repeat. So if you run 400 meters in 72 seconds, you rest 72 seconds when the ratio is 1:1 or twice as long (144 seconds) if it's 1:2.

The rest period is spent jogging or walking to recover. When first starting intervals, use a higher ratio of work effort to rest to ensure completion of the workout.

Stepping Up: Where Do I Go from Here?

When do you know you can run intervals faster? It's tempting to cut your repeat time just a little each week, doing 400-meter repeats in 70 seconds one week, in 68 seconds the next week and then (if you can) in 66 seconds the following week, all keeping the same amount of rest—until illness or injury intervenes. And at that rate, it will.

Instead, first work on reducing the rest period (say from 1:2 to 1:1) before increasing the pace. Increasing the pace too early may result in injury. The goal is to come into a race with the last few weeks of workouts simulating race conditions; that is, faster pace and shorter rest intervals.

Recuperation: How to Keep Coming Back

Speedwork is hard work both physically and psychologically. The increased demands placed on the body by interval training require more time for recovery. Between interval workouts allow at least one day of rest, either easy running or complete rest. Masters runners may need more days to recover. Workouts without adequate rest intervals are an easy way to wear yourself down, resulting in overtraining and even injury.

Schedule speed sessions at least twice a week to get the most benefit from your training. This includes shorter tempo runs, fartlek and time trials, as well as intervals. Remember, if you want to run faster, you have to train faster.

Race Day: Mental Training

Every elite runner has a personal routine to get ready for race day. Much of it is already instilled in the weeks and months of hard

TYPICAL TRAINING SCHEDULE FOR JIM SPIVEY

Jim Spivey, a two-time U.S. Olympian at 1500 meters, has been racing at the international level since 1981. He has done that by incorporating two or three speed sessions per week (when preparing for races), along with recovery days (like Tuesday and Thursday), in his schedule.

Sunday		70–80 min., easy pace
Monday		Long intervals, short rest:
		15 min. warm-up
		10 × 100 m. strides
		6 × 800 m., 400 m. jog between each
		2:11, 2:15, 2:12, 2:09, 2:08, 2:09
		10 min. cooldown
		6 × 100 m. strides
Tuesday	A.M.	25 min., easy
	P.M.	30–35 min., easy
Wednesday		Shorter intervals:
		18 min. warm-up
		10 × 100 m.
		3 sets of 4 × 400 m.
		200 m. jog between each
		400 m. jog between sets
		0:62.3, 0:63.2, 0:62.9, 0:62:3
		0:62.9, 0:63.4, 0:63.3, 0:63:5
		0:63.8, 0:63.1, 0:63.5, 0:63:1 (on roads)
		9 min. cooldown
Thursday	A.M.	25 min., easy
	P.M.	35 min., easy
		10 × 100 m. strides
Friday		20–30 min., easy
		10 × 100 m. strides
Saturday		Race

practice, the conditioning that comes from completing hard workouts and a succession of high-quality weeks.

Most runners, such as Joy Smith, will go out and review the course beforehand. "I want to know where breaks can be made," says Smith. "Knowing that helps me relax during the race because I already have my plans set."

Yet as race day approaches, many elites turn inward; that is, they work on the mental aspects of the race. Here is what three Olympic athletes concentrate on.

Steve Brace plans his success: "I rehearse the possible race situation in my mind, time and time again, leading up to the race. I picture the course, opposition and weather conditions. The more times I go through it, the better prepared I am for the race."

Annette Peters sees the positive side: "I visualize a lot before I get to the starting line. I see myself having a positive race, and I try to put myself in different tactical situations."

PattiSue Plumer cultivates her confidence: "I review race strategy until 24 hours before the race—then I stop. I remember the great training sessions I've had leading up to the race to give me confidence. Then, just before the race, I review my race strategy again."

CHAPTER

21

Marathon Training

AN ELITE MEETING OF THE MINDS

After the 1994 Parkersburg Half-Marathon, some of the best all-time marathoners in the United States sat around a table in a hotel lobby to drink orange juice and soft drinks and talk about marathon training. It was an elite roundtable discussion with the following marathon stars:

Steve Spence: 1991 World Marathon Championships bronze medalist; 1992 Olympic Marathon Trials champ; 2:12:17 personal record (PR).

Kim Jones: 1989 and 1990 runner-up at the New York City Marathon; 1991 and 1993 runner-up at the Boston Marathon; 2:26:40 PR.

Paul Pilkington: 1994 Los Angeles Marathon champ; 1991 Houston Marathon champ; 2:11:13 PR.

Don Janicki: 1987 World Championships marathon team member; 1993 and 1994 Revco/Cleveland Marathon champ; 2:11:16 PR.

The paragraphs in italic explain the physiological rationale behind these athletes' training methods.

Preparation Stages: Putting In the Miles

Q. How long do you train for a marathon? How long is your buildup?

Janicki: About three months is all I can really concentrate on. I pick a marathon and work back 12 weeks from there to set up a training schedule. I'm not one of those people who likes to plan—and train for—a marathon six months or a year in advance. I couldn't stay motivated that long.

Pilkington: I run 8 to 12 weeks of high mileage, then taper. So I train 12 to 14 weeks at the most for a marathon.

Jones: About 16 weeks is right for me. And that means starting off right away with high mileage. All of us are training all the time anyway, so we already have a base and can build from there.

Spence: About 12 weeks works for me, too. But I'll start thinking about it a few weeks before that. At that point I'm doing long, easy runs. Then I start working into it 12 weeks out. Don had a good point—you can't really focus much longer than 12 weeks.

Janicki: Yeah, about 12 weeks or so seems to be where everybody starts from—when you're doing the high mileage plus quality. And like Kim says, we're in shape all the time anyway. It's just a matter of when you start that real tough run for it—that time period when you're really not rested for any other races because you're training hard for a marathon.

Elite runners use three months for fine-tuning their training to meet the marathon challenge; this works for them because they are already highly trained runners. A less trained or less experienced runner may need six months to a year for building up the mileage needed to complete a marathon.

Q. How many miles a week do you run in your buildup phase?

Pilkington: I'm doing 160 right now.

Janicki: I don't go that high, about 100 to 110.

Jones: I do the same as Don. About 100 to 110.

Spence: I like to wait until about six weeks before a marathon, then I get in five good weeks and taper the last week or so. I run in minutes, not miles, and the most I do is about 2½ hours a day.

Pilkington: As far as weekly mileage goes, most of the time I'm around 130 when I'm training for a marathon. This time I have been feeling good and have gone a little bit higher; it wasn't planned that way. I base a lot of my mileage on how I feel recovery-wise. If I feel good, I'll go out and run a little more. If I feel fatigued and tired, I'll back off. I don't necessarily sit down and say, "Okay, I'm going to hit this many miles." It's just what it works out to be.

Just because these elite marathoners are doing 100 miles or more per week doesn't mean it takes that to complete a marathon. Many runners train with less than half those miles and still run successfully. Running 15 to 20 miles per week probably isn't enough, however. Building up to 45 to 50 miles per week over several months and keeping that kind of mileage for four to five weeks prior to tapering will usually be sufficient, as long as finishing is your goal.

When to Take a Break

Q. You wouldn't have any problem with slicing 25 percent from your mileage one week—going from, say, 160 to 120—if you felt tired?

Pilkington: No, I wouldn't. And I do that. I think you need to learn to read your body so that you know when to back off and when to push.

Jones: I take my resting heart rate every morning. When I'm ready for a hard workout, it's 32 to 34; if it's ever over 38, I either take the day off or run easy. Sometimes that happens when I have a long run or a hard speed workout planned. But it doesn't matter, I'll back off anyway.

By monitoring your heart rate, signs of overfatigue can be detected. Your resting heart rate will probably be much higher than Jones's, however. Monitor your heart rate several days to establish a true baseline for you. The key is knowing your body. If you are struggling in your run, maybe it's time to back off. Have flexibility built into your program; don't be overly regimented.

Q. How do you incorporate rest into a 12- to 14-week marathon buildup? Is it planned or does your body tell you when to rest?

Jones: I don't plan it, but I do take a day off now and then.

Spence: I plan to take a day off every two weeks. I usually take off the Monday after a long run.

Janicki: Once a month I take a day off. It's not planned. Usually, my situation is a conflict with family or job. Something is going on and it's not worth it to squeeze in a workout, that extra stress, so I take the day off.

Q. Ever take more than a day off?

Pilkington: If I've gotten to where I need two or three days off, then I've done something wrong. Usually, a day is enough to start feeling strong again.

Jones: When I take more than a day off, I'll take the whole week off. If I need more than one day off, then I've done something wrong—pushed too hard without enough recovery—so I'll take a week's vacation.

Q. You'll take a week off in the middle of marathon training?

Jones: If I need it, yes. It doesn't happen that often, but it has happened. Mentally it's hard. Especially later, when you're on the starting line thinking about your training—and you think about that week off. But you really do become much stronger from the time off, because you build up and avoid breaking down. And that's what marathon training is all about—building yourself up.

Marathon training stresses the body to the limit. A rest day here or there helps to recover glycogen stores depleted during running. Some people require more than one or two days for recovery; don't worry, you won't lose your conditioning in just a few days. The time off will probably improve your training. Having to take several days off every other week, however, may be a sign of too much mileage too quickly.

Long Runs: How Far, How Fast and How Many?

Q. How long is your long run?

Janicki: I'll run 20 to 23 miles.

Pilkington: I'll go 25 miles. I like it because it's 2½ hours of running. I've tried going longer, but I don't like it. Two and a half hours is fine for me. It's about 20 minutes longer than my marathon race time, but I'm running slower.

Jones: I'll run 2½ hours, which is 22 to 23 miles. Once a month, though, I'll run 3 hours, about 26 to 27 miles.

Spence: I like my last long run to be longer than the marathon distance, say 28 to 30 miles, which takes close to three hours. I'll run that about two weeks before the marathon.

Long runs are important to build confidence and to get the body conditioned to burning more fat and less carbohydrates for fuel. Spacing long runs is critical; you need to know your recovery time. Putting these runs too close together could cause problems. Make sure you are well-rested before the next run, especially if the next run is the race.

Q. How fast are your long runs?

Janicki: We have this group workout in Boulder where we go out and start out easy, but by the end it's pretty hard. It's not as hard as marathon race pace. Maybe a 5:30 pace, about 30 seconds per mile slower than marathon race pace.

Pilkington: I try to relax on my long runs. If I'm feeling good, some are a little quicker than others. But long runs don't need to be fast, as long as my other workouts build that quality. If the long runs are too fast, they take too long to recover from. My 2½-hour runs are run about one minute per mile slower than marathon race pace.

Jones: I run my long run easy, too. But I put some tempo in the middle, especially if it's a three-hour run, because I get bored. Every ten minutes I'll surge for three minutes at about marathon pace, then slow the pace down.

Running speed for long runs is relative. You should keep your pace 30 to 60 seconds per mile slower than marathon race pace. This may be eight or nine minutes per mile for less experienced runners.

Q. How many long runs do you do?

Spence: I like to do four or five. I'll start at about 2½ hours, then build up until my last one is 3 hours. Also, I do what I call a medium-long run in the middle of the week where I'll run two hours at a quicker tempo, about 5:30 to 5:40 pace.

Jones: I do what Steve does. I have a shorter long run once a week. I'll run it quick, close to marathon pace. I do that in addition to a long run once a week—unless I'm racing. If I'm racing, I'll put the miles in after the race, during my cooldown jog.

Janicki: I do a weekly long run.

Pilkington: So do I. And I don't back off that much for a race, say a 10-K or a half-marathon, during marathon training. During marathon training, though, I'll cut my long run to 20 miles instead of 25 the week before a race.

Long runs are a fraction of training. If you are doing only 25 to 30 miles per week, a long run may be 10 miles. For most runners, building up to 15 to 20 miles for the long run is sufficient. And you don't have to include long runs every week. Make sure you've recovered from the last one.

Jones: So how close to a race, say a 10-K, do you plan your long run?

Pilkington: Seven days before the race. Even so, it probably hurts the 10-K time. But that's not the main focus—the marathon is.

Q. How close to the marathon is your last long run?

Jones: Two weeks before. And I'll do an easy two-hour run one week before.

Janicki: I like to do my last long run about three weeks out, then a race, preferably a 10-K, two weeks before.

Pilkington: Three to four weeks before the race I'll log my last real long one, then cut it down: 25, then 20, and so on. In the past I've stuck with four weeks, though before Los Angeles I did my last long run three weeks before and it seemed to work well.

Spence: About two weeks before the marathon I do my last long run, which is also my longest training run. Then during the week before I'll run 90 to 100 minutes pretty hard (5:20 pace) as my depletion run.

The key to remember is don't let your last long run hurt your race performance. Be sure to take plenty of time for recovery. Beginners should run their last long run three weeks before the race.

Speedwork: Marathon Speed Sessions

Q. Favorite speed workouts for marathons?

Janicki: I'll run a 3000, then 2 × 2000, then 3 × 1000—at 10-K pace the whole way through. The rest interval between the 3000 and 2000s is a 600-meter jog; I use a 400-meter jog between the 1000s. I'll do that workout one week, alternating with 5 × 2000 or 6 × one mile (with a quarter-mile jog in between) the other weeks. If I can do 6 × one mile at 10-K race pace while still getting in my mileage, I feel pretty ready to run a good marathon.

Pilkington: I like tempo runs. In the middle of a 12-miler, I'll do 5 miles a little faster than marathon race pace. I like the feel and the rhythm tempo runs give you—the same pattern you'll need on marathon race day.

Jones: Because I have asthma, I can push it only so long before I have to recover, so I like shorter intervals: 1000s or 600s. I'll run them at about 10-K pace or a little faster. The quicker running seems to give me a change in leg turnover and keeps my legs sharp for the marathon.

Spence: My bread-and-butter workout leading up to a marathon is 2 × 20 minutes. I'll do it five times before a marathon, once a week. The first time I'll average 5:05 pace, then drop it down about five seconds each time. The last time I'll be close to 4:35 to 4:40 pace, just a bit slower than 10-K race pace. I'll jog 5 minutes in between 20-minute sessions to recover.

Speedwork is important for marathon running. In order to run comfortably at a good pace, you must do one or two sessions per week faster than your race pace.

Tapering

Q. How long do you taper?

Pilkington: I do a four-week taper, cutting back about 10 percent or so each week, maybe a little more. The last week before the marathon I do some light jogging and maybe a light track workout. I don't take the day before a marathon off. I like to keep things loosened up and stretched out. I just feel better when I'm running.

Janicki: Since I don't do as much mileage as Paul does, I usually taper over two weeks. It starts with a race—preferably a 10-K—then I pretty much rest up the last 13 days, dropping mileage, with no heavy intensity. Besides, I don't think there's much you can do two weeks before a marathon that's going to help you at that point. I do short speedwork to sharpen, but nothing taxing. My mileage goes from 110 to 80 or 70 two weeks before; the last week I'll drop it even further. If I feel like it, I may take days off during that time.

Jones: My taper is similar to Don's. I'll try to find a race two to three weeks before a marathon, taper for that race and continue to taper afterward. I'll drop down to 40 miles the week before the marathon—from 110 three weeks before that. If I don't want to go out and run a couple of days before the marathon, I don't. But usually I feel anxious, so I get out there and run a little each day.

Spence: I start about two weeks out, cutting back on my medium-long run and on my easy days (I'll run only once a day instead of twice). I still get the speedwork in that week. Then the week before the marathon I usually take a day off, and on the other days I run minimal mileage.

Tapering is very important for marathon success. Allow one to two weeks for your body to recover from the high training mileage. This allows for complete glycogen storage in the muscles and helps you prepare mentally for the challenge.

The Key to 26.2 Miles

Q. What do you think is *the* key to training for a marathon?

Spence: For me there are three keys: doing the mileage (so that the distance is more comfortable), learning a race pace and locking into that pace during training.

Janicki: I would say consistency. Even when you feel tired, you still have to go out there and train. A lot of people think that when they're tired, they can't train. Of course, if you're breaking down, you need to take the time off. But just being tired is another story. Training when you're tired is what getting ready for a marathon is all about.

Pilkington: Consistency is important. You need to get those long runs in. But I think the taper is also a key. Many people don't give enough attention to the taper. They do their long runs too close to the race itself—or further away from the race but too fast—and on race day they have dead legs. You need to learn to let the body recover and get itself ready for the marathon.

Jones: I agree—consistency and the taper. The taper is critical. And actually there's one other thing: the right attitude. A lot of people get really uptight when they're training hard for a marathon and they run slow at another race, say a 10-K. They get too upset and too worried about that race. They put too much emphasis on it, when they just need to let it go and continue their training. The marathon is the goal.

Janicki: And that's true not only with races leading up to a marathon but with the marathon itself. There are people who put too much emphasis on one marathon. I've seen too many good runners who've run a bad marathon throw their arms up and say, "The marathon isn't for me." Hey, it's only one race. You wouldn't say that about a 10-K after a bad showing. There are plenty of other marathons out there. All you have to do is pick another—then go for it.

Doing the work and consistency are important for any distance. It is important to go into the marathon confident, just as for any other race.

Racing through a Bad Patch

Q. Let's turn to the actual race itself. What do you do about problems during the race? Those bad patches where you feel like dropping out?

Janicki: I usually find that if you stick it out, fighting that feeling that says you should drop out, you come out the better for it. You may not be real pleased with the race, but just by hanging in there and finishing you've accomplished something. There are some bad patches in all marathons; you just have to run through them.

Jones: Once you drop out, it's much easier to drop out the next time, because mentally you're not facing the test of the marathon. Mentally you're breaking down and letting the bad patch get to you.

Janicki: That's why I like doing hard speed workouts with a group. If you're with a group and feeling bad, you don't want to let them get away, so you tuck in and concentrate rather than fall back. It's a lot like the mental discipline you need to use in a marathon.

Strategic Plans: Thinking on Your Feet

Q. Do you have any strategies for racing a marathon?

Janicki: After the "rabbits" drop off, that's where the racing really starts for me. If you're not feeling good then, you're in trouble. I think Steve would disagree with that because he's run races where he's come from way back at the end, but I feel I need to be ready much earlier if I'm going to run a good marathon.

TYPICAL TRAINING SCHEDULE FOR DON JANICKI

When training, Don Janicki, a 2:11 marathoner, combines speedwork with 12 to 20 miles per day for a weekly total of 110 miles.

Sunday	A.M.	20-plus mi., 6:00–7:00 pace, faster at the end
Monday	A.M.	6 mi., 6:00–7:00 pace
	P.M.	7–9 mi., 6:00–7:00 pace
		Weights (upper body only)
Tuesday	A.M.	5–6 mi., 6:30–7:00 pace
	P.M.	Track workout, long interval:
		6 × 1600 m.
		4 × 2000 m.
Wednesday	A.M.	6 mi., 6:00–7:00 pace
	P.M.	6 mi., 6:00–7:00 pace
		Weights (upper body)
Thursday	A.M.	15–18 mi., 6:00–7:00 pace
	P.M.	5 mi., 6:30–7:00 pace
Friday	A.M.	5 mi., 6:00–7:00 pace
	P.M.	Track workout, short intervals:
		12 × 400 m.
		Weights (upper body)
Saturday	A.M.	6–7 mi., 6:30–7:00 pace
	P.M.	6–7 mi., 6:30–7:00 pace

Pilkington: The first thing I have to do is defeat the distance. You have to know your fitness level and what you can run at that level. That's because a marathon is unlike any other race. By that I mean if you misjudge your pace in, say, a 10-K, you might slow down a lot but you'll still finish without too much of a problem. But if you misjudge in a marathon, you really suffer. So you have to get this clear in your mind: What can I do? I know that before I get to the starting line. And in a marathon, more so than any other race, you have to run your own race. I'm not saying that I'll totally disregard the competition, but I have a marathon plan—based on what I know I'm capable of running—and I stick to that plan. I don't let someone else dictate how my race goes. This plan covers the pace for the first part of the race and even things like when I can attack and how soon I can go for it. Stuff like that.

Janicki: You not only have to be able to go for it, you also have to put yourself in a position to go for it.

Spence: I agree. I know my strengths and limitations, so I want to have a plan—or several plans—so I can react to a situation. I have to decide, for example, what I want to do if the pace goes faster than what I want: If it's just a little faster than what I want, I might decide to stay with them instead of dropping back. I make all these decisions before the race even starts.

Jones: Elite women don't seem to run in packs very much, so I've always run my own race. I've never forced my body to do something it wasn't ready to do at the time. So if someone surges nine miles into a marathon and I'm not ready to go with them, I'll let them go. Mentally, I divide the race into three sections. The first ten miles is sort of relaxing, getting into a rhythm—I'm thinking this is really easy, even though I'm running a pretty good pace. During the second ten miles I look for my competition, get focused and get in gear. In the last six miles I go for it! Actually, though, I'm running the same pace with each segment, but these mental strategies help keep me from slowing down, which is the real battle for me in a marathon.

Everyone has his own strategies. But the beginner should just run to finish. Don't get caught up in the excitement. Your first time, finishing is the goal, not a particular time.

Warm-Ups: Less Is Best

Q. What kind of warm-up—if at all—do you do before a marathon?

Spence: A long warm-up isn't necessary for a marathon. I usually jog for about ten minutes and do some strides. Then I'm ready to go.

Jones: I do the same. Sometimes I jog only five minutes. I try not to think too much. I listen to music.

Janicki: I always thought a good rule of thumb is the longer the race, the shorter the warm-up. I just jog for a few minutes.

Pilkington: I do five to six minutes of jogging before a marathon and then some strides. That's it. That's because in the marathon you're concerned with saving up your muscle glycogen stores. So you want to expend as little energy as possible in the warm-up—just enough to get your heart rate up and then back down a little bit, enough to start to break a sweat—in order to conserve the muscle glycogen.

Janicki: I usually find that I'm so excited about the marathon that I don't need that much warm-up anyway.

Jones: Another important time is the first five minutes of the marathon. Those five minutes are critical. You can overdo it in the first five minutes and ruin the rest of your race. So for the first five minutes I really run within myself. I don't want to get my core temperature too high. I don't want to get my heart rate too high. I want to settle in. Then, once that five minutes is past, I decide what I'm going to do.

Pilkington: I think that's key, too, because when you first begin a hard run, the rate at which you're burning glycogen is very high. So if you go out too fast, you're essentially taking the top off your fuel tank right away—and you're setting yourself up for problems later.

The beginner needs little warm-up—do some stretching and start slow so that the early part of the race is a warm-up. Don't get overly excited and blow it the first mile or so by running too fast.

How Many? *Not* Every Sunday

Q. How many marathons can you run a year?

Janicki: I feel that two is all I can handle in a year. It takes a lot out of me, sometimes more emotionally than physically.

Pilkington: Two, but some great marathoners have run three and four. One year, for example, Kim ran marathons one after another.

Jones: In 1989 I ran four marathons. I think I was lucky not to get injured. The first race was January in Houston, then Boston in April where I ran sub-2:30 for the first time. Then I ran Twin Cities in the fall in 2:31, and four weeks later I was second in New York with a 2:27. But I coasted through the Twin Cities Marathon because the next competitor was five minutes behind me, so mentally it didn't take anything out of me. That was a good year for me, but I wouldn't advise four marathons in one year. Two is generally the most for me.

Spence: I think two marathons are about the most anyone should do in a year without running the risk of getting injured or sick.

Jones: For a long marathon career, two a year is the most.

Take it from the elites: Don't overrace. Allow yourself plenty of time to recover both physically and mentally between marathons and your enjoyment will last longer.

CHAPTER

22

Who's Who in Running

LEARN MORE ABOUT OUR TOP RUNNERS

This chapter gives you a closer look at some of the elite runners interviewed for this book—a rundown of their "dossier" includes their personal profile (including height, weight and the number of years they've been running), their running profile, their personal records, a typical training week and their total weekly mileage.

Use this information to spur yourself to greater heights, not to disparage your current level of performance. Many elites believe that a runner's level of motivation can be as important as his or her inborn ability.

What's more, the only competitor who really matters is yourself. In his book *Personal Best,* George Sheehan writes: "A jockey, speaking of a champion horse, said, 'He makes the effort and makes it more often.' The uncrowned champions at the back of the pack do the same. Unconcerned with what others are doing, driven by the need to do our best, we make the effort and make it more often. And for those few moments, we become the equal of anyone on this Earth."

STEVE BRACE

PERSONAL PROFILE

Date of birth	7/7/61
Height/Weight	5'10"/140 lb.
School	Gwent (England)
Occupation	Athlete
Number of years running	12

RUNNING PROFILE

1988	Chicago Marathon, 5th place
1989	Paris Marathon Champion
1990	Paris Marathon Champion
1991	Berlin Marathon Champion
1992	Olympic Marathon, 27th place

PERSONAL RECORDS

400 m.	0:61.4	10,000 m.	29:06.0
800 m.	1:58.0	Half-marathon	62:30.0
1500 m.	3:56.0	Marathon	2:10:57.0
5000 m.	14:12.0		

TYPICAL TRAINING WEEK

Sunday		Race or long run (18–20 mi.)
Monday	A.M.	10 mi.
	P.M.	10 mi. with 8 × 500 m., 80–82 sec., 100 m. jog between each
Tuesday	A.M.	17 mi.
	P.M.	5 mi.
Wednesday	A.M.	5 mi.
	P.M.	11 mi. with 6 × 4 min., 1.5 min. recovery between each
Thursday	A.M.	8 mi.
	P.M.	10 mi.
Friday	A.M.	5 mi.
Saturday	A.M.	3 mi.
	P.M.	3 mi.

BUDD COATES

PERSONAL PROFILE

Date of birth	4/6/57
Height/Weight	5'7"/130 lb.
School	Springfield College
Occupation	Corporate fitness director
Number of years running	21

RUNNING PROFILE

1989	Chemical Bank Corporate Athlete of the Year
1984, 1988, 1992	U.S. Olympic Marathon Trials

PERSONAL RECORDS

400 m.	0:54	10,000 m.	29:01
800 m.	1:57	Half-marathon	63:45
Mile	4:09	Marathon	2:13:02
5000 m.	14:08		

TYPICAL TRAINING WEEK

Sunday		Long run
Monday	A.M.	5 mi., easy
	P.M.	13 mi. (hills)
Tuesday		13–17 mi. (with 40–60 min. at race pace)
Wednesday	A.M.	5 mi., easy
	P.M.	8 mi., easy
Thursday		13–15 mi. with 10 × 100 m.
Friday	A.M.	5 mi., easy
	P.M.	Speed 200s or 100, 200, 300
Saturday		Off

BARB FILUTZE

PERSONAL PROFILE

Date of birth	6/21/46
Height/Weight	5'1½"/100 lb.
School	Villa Maria Academy
Occupation	Coach, shop owner, homemaker
Number of years running	15

RUNNING PROFILE

1984, 1988	U.S. Olympic Marathon Trials
1987	*Runner's World* Racer of the Year

Set 40 U.S. records since 1982, 1 world record, 4 masters records
3-time TAC national masters champion

PERSONAL RECORDS

400 m.	0:72	8000 m.	28:02
800 m.	2:26	10,000 m.	33:36
Mile	5:07	Half-marathon	1:16:00
5000 m.	16:58	Marathon	2:41:18

TYPICAL TRAINING WEEK

Sunday		18 mi.
Monday	A.M.	5 mi., 7:00 pace, 4 strides at end
	P.M.	6 mi., 7:30 pace
		10 × 1 min., hard pace
Tuesday	A.M.	9 mi., 7:30 pace
		4 × 30 sec.
	P.M.	Stationary bike, 15 min.
Wednesday	A.M.	5 mi., easy
	P.M.	5 mi. track workout:
		5 × 200 m., hard, in 600, 800, 1000, 1400, 800
		3 mi., easy
Thursday		12 mi., easy (hills)
Friday	A.M.	3 mi., easy
	P.M.	6 × 3 min.
Saturday		10 mi., easy (grass)

LAURIE GOMEZ-HENES

PERSONAL PROFILE

Date of birth	4/16/70
Height/Weight	5'7"/110 lb.
School	North Carolina State University
Occupation	Graduate student, runner
Number of years running	10

RUNNING PROFILE

1992	U.S. Olympic Trials, 3000 m., 8th place
1992	U.S. Track and Field Championships, 10-K, 5th place
1993	U.S. vs. Great Britain, indoor track
1993	World University Games, 10-K
1995	World Championships, 10,000 m.

8-time all-American

PERSONAL RECORDS

1500 m.	4:22	10,000 m.	31:17
5000 m.	15:49		

TYPICAL TRAINING WEEK

Sunday		5 mi. or rest
Monday	A.M.	4 mi., 6:30 pace
	P.M.	6 mi., 6:30 pace
		Running drills
Tuesday	A.M.	3 mi., 6:30 pace
	P.M.	2 sets of 3 × 1000 m., starting at 3:10 down to 3:05; 200 m. between each, 3 min. between sets
Wednesday	A.M.	8 mi., 6:15 pace
	P.M.	Circuit training
Thursday	A.M.	4 mi., 6:30 pace
	P.M.	6 mi., 6:30 pace
		Running drills
Friday		3 mi. warm-up
		10 × 400 m.; start at 72 sec. down to 68 sec.
		60 sec. recovery between each
Saturday		10–11 mi.

DAN HELD

PERSONAL PROFILE

Date of birth	10/15/65
Height/Weight	5'9"/135 lb.
School	University of Wisconsin at Eau Claire
Occupation	Insurance agent
Number of years running	14

RUNNING PROFILE

1993	Columbus Marathon, 3rd place
1995	U.S. Marathon Championships, 3rd place

PERSONAL RECORDS

10,000 m.	28:56	Marathon	2:13:50
Half-marathon	1:02:46		

TYPICAL TRAINING WEEK

Sunday	A.M.	20–25 mi., then right into the whirlpool for 15 min. and sauna for 10 min.
Monday	A.M.	8 mi.
	P.M.	2 mi. warm-up and cooldown 6 × 1 mi.
Tuesday	A.M.	6 mi.
	P.M.	8 mi.
Wednesday	A.M.	8 mi.
	P.M.	8 mi., followed by whirlpool and sauna
Thursday	A.M.	6 mi.
	P.M.	2 mi. warm-up and cooldown Track workout: repeat 400s and 800s
Friday	A.M.	8 mi.
	P.M.	8 mi.
Saturday	A.M.	8 mi.
	P.M.	8 mi.

STEVE HOLMAN

PERSONAL PROFILE

Date of birth	3/2/70
Height/Weight	6'1½"/148 lb.
School	Georgetown University
Occupation	Runner
Number of years running	10

RUNNING PROFILE

1992	NCAA 1500 m. champion
1992	Big East Athlete of the Year
1992	Olympics, 1500 m.

PERSONAL RECORDS

400 m.	0:48.90	1500 m.	3:34.95
800 m.	1:47.50	Mile	3:52.70
1000 m.	2:19.90	5000 m.	13:47.00

TYPICAL TRAINING WEEK (FALL)

Sunday		Long run, 14–16 mi.
Monday	A.M.	4 mi., 6:00–6:15 pace
	P.M.	8 mi., 6:00–6:15 pace
Tuesday		On grass:
		1 mi., 4:37
		3 × 2 mi., 9:35, 9:25, 9:24
Wednesday		Same as Monday
Thursday		3 mi., 6:00 pace
		2 mi., 9:45
		3 mi., 6:00 pace
Friday		Same as Monday
Saturday		5 × 1200 m.
		3:19, 3:22, 3:23, 3:22, 3:14

JILL HUNTER

PERSONAL PROFILE

Date of birth	10/14/66
Height/Weight	5'7"/115 lb.
School	Rylon Comp (England)
Occupation	Runner
Number of years running	15

RUNNING PROFILE

1988	Olympics, 3000 m.
1992	Olympics, 10,000 m., 10th place
1992	World Women's Cross-Country Championship, 8th place

PERSONAL RECORDS

5000 m.	15:09	10 mi.	31:41
10,000 m.	31:07	25 km.	1:24:00

TYPICAL TRAINING WEEK

Sunday	A.M.	12–15 mi.
	P.M.	3 mi., plus 8 × 100 m. strides
Monday	A.M.	8 mi.
	P.M.	5 mi.
Tuesday	A.M.	5 mi.
	P.M.	3 sets of 5 × 400 m., 200 m. rest between each 400 m. between sets
Wednesday	A.M.	10–12 mi.
	P.M.	3 mi., plus 8 × 100 m. strides
Thursday	A.M.	8 mi.
	P.M.	5 mi.
Friday		Rest
Saturday	A.M.	5 mi.
	P.M.	8 × 11 min.

150 sit-ups, stretching and leg strengthening each day; light weights on arms 4 days a week

JANE HUTCHISON

PERSONAL PROFILE

Date of birth	12/16/45
Height/Weight	5'6"/115 lb.
School	Pittsburg State University
Occupation	Teacher
Number of years running	16

RUNNING PROFILE

1991	American record, marathon, 45-year-olds
1991	Rocket City Marathon masters champion
1991	Ranked 6th masters female runner, *Runner's World*
1991	Tied national 5-K record for 45-year-olds
1992, 1993	TAC 10-K national masters champion

PERSONAL RECORDS

800 m.	2:21	15,000 m.	54:41
Mile	5:03	Half-marathon	1:19:00
5000 m.	17:20	Marathon	2:45:35
10,000 m.	34:40		

TYPICAL TRAINING WEEK

Sunday		6 mi., with 4 mi. at race pace
Monday	A.M.	3 mi., easy
	P.M.	5 mi.
Tuesday	A.M.	3 mi., easy
	P.M.	9 mi.
Wednesday	A.M.	3 mi., easy
	P.M.	5 mi., fartlek
Thursday		Track workout: 16 × 400 m., 75–82 sec.
Friday		5 mi., easy
Saturday		20 mi., easy

DON JANICKI

PERSONAL PROFILE

Date of birth	4/23/60
Height/Weight	5'10"/135 lb.
School	University of Arizona
Occupation	Account executive, professional runner
Number of years running	17

RUNNING PROFILE

1993, 1994   Revco Marathon champion
NCAA All-American

PERSONAL RECORDS

400 m.	0:56.00	5000 m.	13:44.20
800 m.	1:58.00	10,000 m.	28:26.00
1500 m.	3:46.00	Half-marathon	1:03:15.00
Mile	4:09.00	Marathon	2:11:16.00

TYPICAL TRAINING WEEK

Sunday		20 mi., 6:00–7:00 min., faster at end
Monday	A.M.	6 mi., 6:00–7:00 pace
	P.M.	7–9 mi., 6:00–7:00 pace
Tuesday	A.M.	5–6 mi., 6:30–7:00 pace
	P.M.	Track, long interval:
		6 × 1600 m.
		4 × 2000 m.
Wednesday	A.M.	6 mi., 6:00–7:00 pace
	P.M.	6 mi., 6:00–7:00 pace, weights
Thursday	A.M.	15–18 mi., 6:00–7:00 pace
	P.M.	5 mi., 6:30–7:00 pace
Friday	A.M.	5 mi., 6:00-7:00 pace
	P.M.	Track, short interval:
		12 × 400 m., weights
Saturday	A.M.	6–7 mi., 6:30–7:00 min.
	P.M.	6–7 mi., 6:30–7:00 min.

LYNN JENNINGS

PERSONAL PROFILE

Date of birth	7/1/60
Height/Weight	5'5"/113 lb.
Schools	Princeton University; Harvard University
Occupation	Athlete
Number of years running	20

RUNNING PROFILE

1988	Olympics, 10,000 m.
1990, 1991, 1992	World cross-country champion
1990	Jesse Owens Award winner
1992	Olympics 10,000 m., bronze medalist
1993	Undefeated in road racing

American indoor 3000 m. record (8:40.45), 5000 m. record (15:22.64)
American 10,000 m. record (31:19)

PERSONAL RECORDS

400 m.	0:56.00	5000 m.	15:07.92
800 m.	2:06.00	10,000 m. (road)	31:06.00
1500 m.	4:06.40	(track)	31:19.89
Mile	4:24.14	15,000 m.	49:47.00
2 mi.	9:28.15	10 mi.	52:53.00

TYPICAL TRAINING WEEK

Sunday	14–16 mi., 6:10–6:15 pace
Monday	2 runs totaling 8–10 mi.
Tuesday	2 runs totaling 10–12 mi.
Wednesday	Track workout:
	400 m., 0:68
	1600 m., 4:55
	400 m., 0:68
	1600 m., 4:53
	400 m., 0:68
	1600 m., 4:50
	400 m., 0:66
Thursday	2 runs totaling 12–14 mi.
Friday	4–6 mi., easy pace
Saturday	Race

BOB KENNEDY

PERSONAL PROFILE

Date of birth	8/18/70
Height/Weight	6'0"/148 lb.
School	Indiana University
Occupation	Runner
Number of years running	9

RUNNING PROFILE

1988, 1992	NCAA cross-country champion
1990	NCAA 1500 m. champion
1991	NCAA mile champion
1991	World Championships, 5000 m., 12th place
1992	Olympics, 5000 m., 12th place

20 individual Big Ten titles

PERSONAL RECORDS

400 m.	0:50.00	3000 m.	7:38.45
800 m.	1:50.10	5000 m.	13:14.91
1500 m.	3:38.30	10,000 m.	29:20.00
Mile	3:56.00	(cross-country)	

TYPICAL TRAINING WEEK

Sunday		12 mi., gentle (6:00–6:30 pace)
Monday	A.M.	5 mi., gentle
	P.M.	Road run 15-K, mile splits
		5:05, 5:15, 4:59, 5:12, 4:19,
		5:08, 5:25, 4:51, 5:10
		Total time 47:12
		1 mi. cooldown

Tuesday	A.M.	6 mi., gentle
	P.M.	5 mi., gentle
Wednesday	A.M.	4 mi., gentle
	P.M.	Track workout:
		3 mi. warm-up
		5 × 800 m., 2:08, 2:07, 2:06, 2:02, 2:04
		1:40 rest between each
		2 mi. cooldown
Thursday	A.M.	5 mi., gentle
	P.M.	7 mi., gentle
Friday	A.M.	4 mi., gentle
	P.M.	4 mi., gentle
Saturday	A.M.	2 mi., gentle
	P.M.	Race, 3000 m., 7:44.93
		4 mi. cooldown

DEBBI KILPATRICK-MORRIS

PERSONAL PROFILE

Date of birth	9/9/63
Height/Weight	5'5"/110 lb.
School	Southeast Missouri State College
Occupation	Runner
Number of years running	17

RUNNING PROFILE

1994	Twin Cities Marathon, 3rd place
1995	U.S. National Marathon Championships winner

PERSONAL RECORDS

10,000 m.	33:34	Marathon	2:34:42
Half-marathon	1:13:20		

TYPICAL TRAINING WEEK

Sunday		45 min. (7:00 pace)
Monday		45 min. (7:00 pace)
Tuesday	A.M.	40 min. (6:30 pace), indoors if very cold
	P.M.	20 min. warm-up; alternating 800s (2:35), with 400s (72 sec.) with a 400 recovery jog between each, repeat sequence four times; 20 min. cooldown
Wednesday		45 min. (7:00 pace), indoors if very cold
Thursday	A.M.	40 min. (6:30 pace)
	P.M.	20 min. warm-up; 6 × 5 min. (5:35–5:40 pace) with 2 min. recovery jogs; 20 min. cooldown
Friday		45 min. (7:00 pace)
Saturday	A.M.	Long run for 2:40, leaving water bottles in car parked along bike trail
	P.M.	40 min. (6:30 pace)

JANIS KLECKER

PERSONAL PROFILE

Date of birth	7/18/60
Height/Weight	5'6"/114 lb.
School	University of Minnesota
Occupation	Dentist
Number of years running	14

RUNNING PROFILE

1991, 1992	Twin Cities Marathon champion
1992	U.S. Olympic Marathon Trials champion

PERSONAL RECORDS

5000 m.	15:59	Marathon	2:30:12
10,000 m.	31:44	50-K	3:13:51
Half-marathon	1:10:41		

TYPICAL TRAINING WEEK

Sunday		22–26 mi.
		30-min. pool run
Monday	A.M.	6 mi.
	P.M.	Cross-train (bike, stairs, weights)
Tuesday	A.M.	10–12 mi. and hill repeats
	P.M.	Swim, 1 mi.
Wednesday	A.M.	10 mi.
	P.M.	Bike, stairs, weights
Thursday	A.M.	8–12 mi., speedwork
		Repeat quarters and mi.
	P.M.	Aqua jogging
Friday		15 mi., easy pace
Saturday	A.M.	4–6 mi., easy
	P.M.	Bike

ANNE MARIE LAUCK

PERSONAL PROFILE

Date of birth	3/7/69
Height/Weight	5′6″/105 lb.
School	Rutgers University
Occupation	Athlete
Number of years running	10

RUNNING PROFILE

1991	World University Games 10,000 m. champion
1991, 1993, 1995	World Championships Team
1992	World Cup Team, 10,000 m.
1993	U.S. Nationals, 10,000 m., 2nd place
1993	World Cross-Country Team

4th fastest all-time in 10,000 m. (31:37)
Ranked in top 5 in world for road racing

PERSONAL RECORDS

400 m.	0:60		5000 m.	15:32
800 m.	2:08		10,000 m.	31:47
1500 m.	4:18		Half-marathon	1:12:03
Mile	4:38			

TYPICAL TRAINING WEEK

Sunday		12–14 mi., average 6:00–6:50 pace
Monday	A.M.	8 mi., training pace (6:10–6:40)
	P.M.	5 mi., training pace
Tuesday	A.M.	5–7 mi., training pace
	P.M.	Track workout:
		3–4 × 1 mi., 4:50–4:55 pace
		400 m. jog between each

Wednesday	A.M.	5 mi., easy (6:30 pace)
	P.M.	5 mi., easy
Thursday	A.M.	5–7 mi., training pace
	P.M.	Track workout:

3 sets of 4 × 400 m., 65–68 sec.

200 m. jog between each, 400 m. jog between sets

4 × 200 m., 29–30 sec., 200 m. jog between each

Friday	A.M.	8 mi., easy
	P.M.	May run another 5–7 mi.
Saturday	A.M.	10 mi. with fartlek of 5 min. hard pickups, 2 min. easy between
	P.M.	5 mi. easy, depending on mileage for the week

LORRAINE MOLLER

PERSONAL PROFILE

Date of birth	6/1/55
Height/Weight	5′9″/122 lb.
School	Otago University (New Zealand)
Occupation	Athlete
Number of years running	25

RUNNING PROFILE

1984	Boston Marathon champion
1984	Olympic Marathon, 5th place
1992	Olympic Marathon, bronze medalist

PERSONAL RECORDS

800 m.	2:03.6	10,000 m. (road)	32:08.0
1500 m.	4:10.3	(track)	32:23.0
Mile	4:32.9	15-K	49:08.0
5000 m.	15:32.0	Marathon	2:28:17.0

TYPICAL TRAINING WEEK

Sunday		2½ hr., easy (7:00 pace)
Monday	A.M.	40 min., easy
	P.M.	60 min., easy
Tuesday	A.M.	40 min., easy
	P.M.	3 mi. warm-up
		6 × 1000 m., average 3:14
		3 mi. cooldown
Wednesday		14 mi., 1½ hr.
Thursday	A.M.	40 min., easy
	P.M.	3 mi. warm-up
		8 × 400 m., average 71 sec.
		400 m. jog between each
		3 mi. cooldown
Friday		60 min., easy
Saturday	A.M.	40 min., easy
	P.M.	3 mi. warm-up
		5-K, steady pace, 16:25
		3 mi. cooldown

CATHY O'BRIEN

PERSONAL PROFILE

Date of birth	7/19/67
Height/Weight	5'2"/105 lb.
School	University of New Hampshire
Occupation	Athlete
Number of years running	13

RUNNING PROFILE

1988, 1992	Olympic Marathon
1991	Los Angeles Marathon champion

PERSONAL RECORDS

800 m.	2:12.0 (in workout)	10 mi.	51:47.0
5000 m.	16:00.0	15-K	49:08.0
5 mi.	25:29.0	Half-marathon	1:09:00.0
10,000 m.	31:47.0	Marathon	2:29:00.0

TYPICAL TRAINING WEEK

Sunday		16–25 mi.
Monday	A.M.	10 mi., 6:45 pace
	P.M.	5 mi., easy (7:00 pace)
Tuesday	A.M.	10 mi., 1–2 min. pickups on road
	P.M.	5 mi., easy
Wednesday		16 mi., 6:30 pace
Thursday		6 mi., easy (rest day)
Friday		6 mi., easy (rest day)
Saturday		Race 10-K

SONIA O'SULLIVAN

PERSONAL PROFILE

Date of birth	11/28/69
Height/Weight	5'9"/120 lb.
School	Villanova University
Occupation	Athlete
Number of years running	10

RUNNING PROFILE

1990, 1991	NCAA cross-country champion
1990, 1991	NCAA 3000 m. champion
1991	NCAA 5000 m. champion (indoors)
1992	Olympics, 3000 m., 4th place
1992	World Cross-Country Championships, 7th place
1993	World Championships: 1500 m., 2nd place
	3000 m., 4th place

Irish record holder in 1500 m., mile, 3000 m. and 5000 m.
NCAA 1500 m. record (4:05)
NCAA 5000 m. indoor record (15:17)

PERSONAL RECORDS

800 m.	2:03.30		3000 m.	8:28.00
1500 m.	3:59.41		5000 m.	14:45.00
Mile	4:22.00			

TYPICAL TRAINING WEEK

Sunday	A.M.	35 min., easy
	P.M.	20 × 200 m. (30–32 sec.) or 10 × 300 m. (48 sec.)
Monday	A.M.	45 min., easy
	P.M.	35–45 min., easy
		Plyometrics

Tuesday	A.M.	3 × 1000 m., 600 m., 400 m.
		1000 m. under 2:50
		600 m. under 1:40
		400 m. in 60 sec.
	P.M.	4–5 mi., easy
Wednesday	A.M.	25 min., easy (with strides)
		Plyometrics
	P.M.	35–45 min., easy
Thursday		35 min., easy
Friday		Race 1500 m. or 5000 m.
Saturday		60–70 min., easy

Continue to lift weights throughout season (twice a week)

ANNETTE PETERS

PERSONAL PROFILE

Date of birth	5/31/65
Height/Weight	5'5"/110 lb.
School	University of Oregon
Occupation	First-grade teacher
Number of years running	13

RUNNING PROFILE

1988	NCAA 5000 m. champion
1991	World Team, 3000 m.
1992	Olympics, 3000 m.
1993	American record holder, 5000 m.
1993	1500 m. and 3000 m. national champion
1993	U.S.A. World Cross-Country Trials champion
1993	World Championships, 1500 m. and 3000 m.

PERSONAL RECORDS

800 m.	2:05.90	3000 m.	8:42.09
1500 m.	4:08.87	5000 m.	14:56.07
2000 m.	5:38.80	10,000 m. (road)	31:47.00

TYPICAL TRAINING WEEK

Sunday	50–60 min., easy (7:00 pace)
Monday	7 mi., easy
Tuesday	Track workout:
	3 × 800 m., 2:23, 400 m. jog/walk between each
	3 × 400 m., 0:68, 400 m. jog/walk between each
	3 × 200 m., 0:32, 200 m. jog/walk between each
Wednesday	7 mi., easy
Thursday	3 × 1 mi., 5:30 pace
	4 × 150 m., float, fast, float
Friday	6 mi., easy
Saturday	Track workout:
	600 m., 400 m. rest
	400 m., 600 m. rest
	300 m., 500 m. rest

PATTISUE PLUMER

PERSONAL PROFILE

Date of birth	4/27/62
Height/Weight	5'4"/112 lb.
Schools	Stanford University; Stanford Law School
Occupation	Mom, runner, lawyer
Number of years running	15

RUNNING PROFILE

1988	Olympics, 3000 m.
1990	Fifth Avenue Mile champion
1990	Track and Field New Athlete of the Year
1992	Olympics, 1500 m., 10th place and 3000 m., 5th place

American record, 5000 m.
Collegiate record holder in 3000 m., 5000 m. and indoor 3-K
2-time NCAA champion
2-time member U.S. Olympic Team, Olympic finalist
5-time national champion

PERSONAL RECORDS

400 m.	0:56		Mile	4:16
800 m.	2:00		3000 m.	8:40
1500 m.	4:03		5000 m.	15:00

TYPICAL TRAINING WEEK

Sunday	Long run
Monday	2 sets of 4 × 400 m., 58–62 sec.
	1–2 laps jog for recovery between each,
	1 mi. between sets
Tuesday	30–45 min. easy run, 15–20 min. for striding
Wednesday	8–12 × 100 m., 13–14 sec., 300 m. between each
Thursday	Rest
Friday	20 min., with 10 min. of striding
Saturday	Race

KEN POPEJOY

PERSONAL PROFILE

Date of birth	12/9/50
Height/Weight	5'8"/135 lb.
School	Michigan State University
Occupation	Lawyer
Number of years running	30

RUNNING PROFILE

1972	U. S. Olympic Trials, 800 m. and 1500 m., semifinalist
1973	Big Ten outdoor mile champion
1975	AAU Championships, 1500 m., 2nd place
1976	Olympic Trials, 1500 m., finalist
1991, 1993	World masters champion, 1500 m.

American masters record holder: 800 m. (indoor), 1:55.41;
800 m. (outdoor), 1:52.50; 1500 m. (indoor), 3:56.70;
Mile (indoor), 4:14.41; 3000 m. (indoor), 8:43.90

PERSONAL RECORDS

400 m.		0:47.2	Mile		3:57.0
	(masters)	0:51.1		(masters)	4:08.8
800 m.		1:47.2	Half-marathon		1:09:00.0
	(masters)	1:52.5	Marathon		2:34:04.0
1500 m.		3:38.4			
	(masters)	3:51.5			

TYPICAL TRAINING WEEK

Sunday	Long run, 70–85 min., (6:40–7:00 pace)
Monday	Track workout, long intervals: 800 m., 1320 m.
Tuesday	40 min., easy run 10 strides
Wednesday	Track workout, short intervals: 200–600 m. repeats
Thursday	30–35 min., easy run Easy strides
Friday	25 min., easy run 10 strides
Saturday	Competition

REUBEN REINA

PERSONAL PROFILE

Date of birth	11/16/67
Height/Weight	5'7"/124 lb.
School	University of Arkansas
Occupation	Runner
Number of Years Running	10

RUNNING PROFILE

1991	World Championships, 5000 m.
1992	Olympics, 5000 m.

2-time NCAA indoor 3000 m. champion
8-time all-American

PERSONAL RECORDS

400 m.	0:51.00	Mile	3:57.01
800 m.	1:52.00	5000 m.	13:24.00
1500 m.	3:40.00	10,000 m.	28:50.00

TYPICAL TRAINING WEEK

Sunday		14 mi., 6:00 pace
Monday	A.M.	4–5 mi., 6:00–6:30 pace
	P.M.	4 × 1 mi., 4:15–4:20 pace
		3 min. jog between each
		2 mi. warm-up and cooldown
Tuesday	A.M.	4–5 mi., 6:00–6:30 pace
	P.M.	8–10 mi., weights
Wednesday	A.M.	4–5 mi., 6:00–6:30 pace
	P.M.	16 × 400 m., 61–64 sec.
		60 sec. jog between each
		2 mi. warm-up and cooldown
Thursday	A.M.	4–5 mi., 6:00–6:30 pace
	P.M.	6–8 mi., weights
Friday	A.M.	2 mi.
	P.M.	4 mi., easy (6:30–7:00 pace)
Saturday		If not racing, run 10 mi. on Friday or track workout on Saturday

NICK ROSE

PERSONAL PROFILE

Date of birth	12/30/51
Height/Weight	5'9"/132 lb.
School	Western Kentucky University
Occupation	Runner
Number of years running	26

RUNNING PROFILE

1980, 1984	Olympics, 10,000 m.
1994	Masters champion in the Bloomsday 15-K (Spokane, WA), Charlotte 10-K (Charlotte, NC), London Marathon, New York City Marathon, Revco Cleveland 10-K, Steamboat 4-Mile (Peoria, IL)

3-time NCAA champion

PERSONAL RECORDS

800 m.	1:51.0	5000 m.	13:18.0
1500 m.	3:40.6	10,000 m.	27:31.0
Mile	3:57.6	Half-marathon	60:03.0
3000 m.	7:40.4		

TYPICAL TRAINING WEEK

Sunday	A.M.	10 mi., 6:30 pace
Monday	A.M.	5 mi., 6:30 pace
	P.M.	5 mi., 6:30 pace
Tuesday	A.M.	10 mi., 6:30 pace
Wednesday	A.M.	5 mi., 6:30 pace
	P.M.	Hill session: 12 × 300 m. or 12 × 400 m. on grass
Thursday	A.M.	5 mi., 6:30 pace
	P.M.	5 mi., 6:30 pace
Friday	A.M.	5 mi., 6:30 pace
	P.M.	5 mi., 6:30 pace
Saturday		Race or 6 × 800 m. on grass or 5 × 1200 m. on grass

RIC SAYRE

PERSONAL PROFILE

Date of birth	8/9/53
Height/Weight	5'10"/136 lb.
School	Walsh University
Occupation	Business owner
Number of years running	27

RUNNING PROFILE

1983   Los Angeles Marathon Champion
2-time NAIA All-American, cross-country

PERSONAL RECORDS

1500 m.	3:59	10 mi.	48:29
Mile	4:17	20,000 m.	60:50
10,000 m.	29:21	Half-marathon	64:43
15,000 m.	44:46	Marathon	2:12:59

TYPICAL TRAINING WEEK

Sunday	A.M.	18–20 mi., easy
Monday	A.M.	7–10 mi., easy
Tuesday	A.M.	13 mi., easy
	P.M.	90 min. mountain bike ride
Wednesday	A.M.	5–7 mi., easy
	P.M.	3 mi. warm-up
		6 × 400 m., 200 m. rest between each
		2 mi. cooldown
Thursday	A.M.	10 mi., easy
	P.M.	60 min. mountain bike ride
Friday	A.M.	7–10 mi.
Saturday		Race or tempo run of 8-K to half-marathon

BOB SCHLAU

PERSONAL PROFILE

Date of birth	9/28/47
Height/Weight	5'7"/126 lb.
Schools	Denison University; Ohio State University
Occupation	Financial consultant
Number of years running	30

RUNNING PROFILE

1984	U.S. Olympic Marathon Trials
1988	U.S. Olympic Marathon Trials
1988	Ranked 1st masters runner in the world
1989	Ranked 2nd masters runner in the world
1993	South Carolina Athletic Hall of Fame

National marathon champion

PERSONAL RECORDS

400 m.	0:52		10,000 m.	30:26
800 m.	2:01		Half-marathon	66:51
Mile	4:16		Marathon	2:17:16
5000 m.	14:32			

TYPICAL TRAINING WEEK

Sunday		Long run (12–18 mi.) with some easy pickups; during marathon training, long run goes to 16–20 mi.
Monday		8 mi., easy (6:50 pace)
Tuesday	A.M.	Track workout:
		5 × 1 mi. at 4:55 pace or 16 × 400 m., 69–70 sec.
	P.M.	4 mi., easy
Wednesday		8–9 mi.; 5 easy, last 4 accelerations or fartlek; during marathon preparation the run goes to 11–12 mi.
Thursday		8 mi., easy
Friday		8 mi., easy
Saturday	A.M.	Track workout:
		Long warm-up
		3 mi. time trial
		15:10–15:20

JON SINCLAIR

PERSONAL PROFILE

Date of birth	10/4/57
Height/Weight	5'7"/128 lb.
School	Colorado State University
Occupation	Runner
Number of Years Running	20

RUNNING PROFILE

1979	NCAA All-American, cross-country, indoor mile
1979	USTFA All-American, 1500 m.
1980	TAC national cross-country champion
1984	Olympic Trials, 5000 m. and 10,000 m.
1984	TAC national 10,000 m. champion
1988, 1992	U.S. Olympic Marathon Trials

PERSONAL RECORDS

400 m.	0:51		5000 m.	13:35
1500 m.	3:45		10,000 m.	28:16
Mile	4:03		Marathon	2:13:29

TYPICAL TRAINING WEEK

Sunday		1½–2½ hour run
Monday	A.M.	5 mi., easy
	P.M.	5 mi., easy
Tuesday	A.M.	10 mi., steady (5:30–5:45 pace)
	P.M.	2 mi. warm-up
		14 × 200 m., 33–35 sec., 200 m. jog between each
		2 mi. cooldown
Wednesday	A.M.	10 mi., easy
	P.M.	5 mi., easy
Thursday	A.M.	12 mi., gradual uphill at 6:00 pace, then 3 mi. downhill at 5:10 pace
Friday	A.M.	10 mi., easy
	P.M.	5 mi., easy
Saturday	A.M.	2 mi. warm-up
		5 × 1000 m., 2:55, 200 m. jog between each
		2 mi. cooldown
	P.M.	5 mi., easy

JOY SMITH

PERSONAL PROFILE

Date of birth	1/5/62
Height/Weight	5'5"/105 lb.
Schools	Air Force Academy; University of Kansas
Occupation	Athlete
Number of years running	9

RUNNING PROFILE

1983	All-American, 800 m. and 1500 m.
1988	U.S. Olympic Marathon Trials
1991	U.S. World Cup Team: 15-K, marathon
1992	U.S. Olympic Trials, 6th place
1993	Boston Marathon, 3rd place
1993	USTF Half-Marathon Championships, 2nd place

PERSONAL RECORDS

400 m.	0:58	10,000 m.	32:08
800 m.	2:09	12,000 m.	41:44
Mile	4:36	15,000 m.	51:00
5000 m.	16:15	Half-marathon	1:11:43
8000 m.	26:51	Marathon	2:34:20

TYPICAL TRAINING WEEK

Sunday	A.M.	22 mi. on trails
Monday	A.M.	6 mi., 7:00 pace
	P.M.	18 min. warm-up
		4 × 1 mi., 5:12–5:16 pace
		15 min. cooldown
Tuesday	A.M.	4 mi., 7:00 pace
	P.M.	12 mi., with 2 × 6 min. pickup at 5:30 pace
Wednesday	A.M.	6 mi., 7:00 pace
	P.M.	18 min. warm-up
		4 × 400 m., 70–72 sec., 30 sec. rest between each
		15 min. cooldown
Thursday	A.M.	9 mi., 7:00 pace
Friday	A.M.	Recovery day, 30 min.
Saturday	A.M.	10 mi., 6:30 pace

STEVE SPENCE

PERSONAL PROFILE

Date of birth	5/8/62
Height/Weight	5'9"/135 lb.
School	Shippensburg University
Occupation	Runner
Number of years running	17

RUNNING PROFILE

1984	NCAA 5000 m. champion
1985	NCAA indoor 5000 m. champion
1989, 1990, 1991	TAC Distance Runner of the Year
1991	World Marathon Championships, bronze medalist
1992	Olympic Marathon

American record holder: 12,000 m. (34:19), 15,000 m. (42:40)

7-time all-American, NCAA Division II

PERSONAL RECORDS

400 m.	0:51	10,000 m. (road)	27:51
800 m.	1:55	12,000 m.	34:19
1500 m.	3:48	15,000 m.	42:40
Mile	4:04	Half-marathon	62:09
5000 m.	13:42	Marathon	2:12:17

TYPICAL TRAINING WEEK

Sunday		Long run, 1½–2 hr., 5:50–6:15 pace
Monday	A.M.	30 min., easy
	P.M.	60 min. (6:20 pace or rest day every 2 weeks)
Tuesday		Hill repeats, track session or road fartlek
Wednesday		45–70 min. (6:30–6:45 pace)
Thursday	A.M.	40 min., easy
	P.M.	50 min. (6:30 pace)
Friday		Hill repeats, track session or road fartlek
Saturday	A.M.	30 min., easy
	P.M.	60 min., easy

JIM SPIVEY

PERSONAL PROFILE

Date of birth   3/7/60
Height/Weight   5'10"/137 lb.
School   Indiana University
Occupation   Athlete
Number of years running 18

RUNNING PROFILE

1981   U.S.A. vs. U.S.S.R., 1500 m. champion
1981   World Student Games, 1500 m., 4th place
1982   National Sports Festival, 5000 m. champion
1983   U.S.A. vs. Nordic, 1500 m. champion
1983   World Championships, 5000 m., 9th place
1984   U.S. Olympic Trials, 1500 m. champion
1984   Olympics, 1500 m., 5th place
1985   U.S.A. vs. England (indoor), mile champion
1985   U.S.A. vs. England, 3000 m., 3rd place
1986   Goodwill Games, 1500 m., 4th place
1987   Pan American Games, 1500 m., 2nd place
1987   World Championships, 1500 m., 3rd place
1988   U.S. Olympic Trials, 1500 m., 4th place
1992   U.S. Olympic Trials, 1500 m. champion
1992   Olympics, 1500 m., 8th place
1993   World Championships, 1500 m., 5th place

PERSONAL RECORDS

400 m.	0:48.90	2000 m.	4:52.44*
800 m.	1:46.50	3000 m.	7:37.04
1500 m.	3:31.01	5000 m.	13:19.24
Mile	3:49.80	10,000 m.	29:05.00

*American record

TYPICAL TRAINING WEEK

Sunday		70–80 min., easy pace
Monday		Long intervals, short rest:
		15 min. warm-up
		10 × 100 m.
		6 × 800 m., 400 m. jog between each
		2:11, 2:15, 2:12, 2:09, 2:08, 2:09
		10 min. cooldown
		6 × 100 m.
Tuesday	A.M.	25 min., easy
	P.M.	30–35 min., easy
Wednesday		Shorter intervals:
		18 min. warm-up
		10 × 100 m.
		3 sets of 3 × 400 m.
		200 m. jog between each
		400 m. jog between sets
		0:62.3, 0:63.2, 0:62.9
		0:62.9, 0:63.4, 0:63.3
		0:63.8, 0:63.1, 0:63.5 (on roads)
		9 min. cooldown
Thursday	A.M.	25 min., easy
	P.M.	35 min., easy
		10 × 100 m.
Friday		20–30 min., easy
		10 × 100 m.
Saturday		Race

LISA WEIDENBACH

PERSONAL PROFILE

Date of birth	12/13/61
Height/Weight	5'10"/128 lb.
School	University of Michigan
Occupation	Athlete
Number of years running	12

RUNNING PROFILE

1983	NCAA All-American, 10,000 m.
1984, 1988, 1992	U.S. Olympic Team alternate, Marathon
1985	Boston Marathon champion
1989	Track and Field New Runner of the Year
1993	Twin Cities Marathon champion

PERSONAL RECORDS

Mile	4:36	10 mi.	52:32
5000 m.	15:32	Half-marathon	1:10:07
8000 m.	25:32	30,000 m.	1:43:26*
10,000 m.	31:34	Marathon	2:28:15
15,000 m.	48:28*		

*American record

TYPICAL TRAINING WEEK

Sunday		20–22 mi., 30–40 sec. slower than marathon race pace
Monday	A.M.	4 mi.
	P.M.	8 mi.
Tuesday		3 mi. warm-up
		5 × 1 mi. on track, 40-45 sec. faster than marathon pace
		200 m. jog or 90 sec. between each
		3 mi. cooldown

Wednesday		9 mi., easy
Thursday	A.M.	6 mi.
	P.M.	6 mi.
Friday		3 mi. warm-up
		5 mi. control run, 20–30 sec. faster than marathon pace
		3 mi. cooldown
Saturday	A.M.	6 mi.
	P.M.	6 mi.

TODD WILLIAMS

PERSONAL PROFILE

Date of birth	3/7/69
Height/Weight	5'8"/130 lb.
School	University of Tennessee
Occupation	Runner
Number of years running	10

RUNNING PROFILE

1992	Olympics, 10,000 m., 10th place
1995	Jacksonville River Run 15-K champion (American record)

PERSONAL RECORDS

10,000 m.	27:40	Half-marathon	1:00:11

TYPICAL TRAINING WEEK

Sunday	A.M.	5 mi.
	P.M.	3 mi. warm-up
		8 × 800 m. on grass with 2 min. recovery jogs (first 400 m. is run at a hard effort, up a slight incline, to simulate the start of a race)
		3 mi. cooldown
Monday	A.M.	5 mi.
	P.M.	"Doug Brown 10" (hilly 10-miler at 5:10 pace)
Tuesday	A.M.	5 mi.
	P.M.	8–10 mi. (recovery day)
Wednesday	A.M.	5 mi.
	P.M.	8 mi.

Thursday	A.M.	5 mi.
	P.M.	2 mi. warm-up
		4 × 250 m. hill
		"The wheel"—9 × 200 m. grass hill
		Finish with 2 × 400 m. (hard) on the track
		2 mi. cooldown
Friday	A.M.	5 mi.
	P.M.	8–10 mi. (recovery day)
Saturday	A.M.	5 mi.
	P.M.	10 mi., average 6:00 pace

About the Authors

Ken Sparks, Ph.D., is associate professor in exercise physiology and health at Cleveland State University. He received his bachelor of science and master of science degrees from Ball State University in Muncie, Indiana, and his doctor of philosophy degree from Indiana University in Bloomington. Dr. Sparks has published many research articles on the topics of exercise performance and fitness and is also the author of *The Long-Distance Runners' Guide to Training and Racing*.

Dr. Sparks is a former All-American in track and a world-class middle-distance runner. Currently, he is an elite masters runner at distances ranging from 800 meters to the marathon and holds several age-group world and American records. Dr. Sparks has been named Runner of the Year by TAC for both long-distance running and track for ages 45 to 49. Dr. Sparks was a silver medalist at the world Veterans Games in both the 800 and 1500 meters for ages 50 to 55. He lives in Chagrin Falls, Ohio.

Dave Kuehls has been a senior writer at *Runner's World* magazine since 1992. Kuehls also writes for *Sports Illustrated, GQ, Outside* and *Track and Field News*. He lives in Akron, Ohio.

Index